TOFU

A NEW WAY TO HEALTHY EATING

TOFU
A NEW WAY TO HEALTHY EATING

LINDA LEE BARBER
&
JUNKO LAMPERT

Windward

This edition published 1986 for Portland House/Windward
by Century Hutchinson Ltd
Brookmount House,
62-65 Chandos Place
London WC2N 4NW

Based on The Tofu Gourmet, published by
Shofunotomo Co., Ltd.,
2-9 Kanda Surugadai, Chiyoda-ku, Tokyo 101, Japan

ISBN 0-7126-1103-7

Measures for ingredients are given in both metric and
imperial measures. Do not mix the use of the two.

Edited, designed and produced by The Paul Press Ltd,
22 Bruton Street, London W1X 7DA

Project Editor Rachel Warren
Art Editor Joanna Walker

Art Director Stephen McCurdy
Editorial Director Jeremy Harwood
Publishing Director Nigel Perryman

Typeset by Wordsmiths, Street, Somerset
Origination by Gee & Watson, Sutton, Surrey
Printed and bound in the Netherlands by Royal Smeets
Offset BV, Weert

CONTENTS

INTRODUCTION

W hat do you look for in a cookbook? Mouth-watering recipes, party ideas, luscious lovely desserts? If so, health food is probably not among your first priorities – unless, that is, you are among the health food gurus who insist on such fare as live yoghurt and organically grown fruit and vegetables.

We should all be concerned about our health to some degree, however. And bombarded as we are today with dietary tips, most people recognize that the idea of good nutrition is medically sound. The task is how to make healthy eating not so much a chore as an epicurean delight.

This is what this book is all about. It presents a glorious range of dishes suited to every occasion. There are eye-catching appetizers and tasty party dips, exotic main meals and light, creamy desserts. But what makes each recipe highly and healthily nutritious is the inclusion of tofu and its by-products in the ingredients.

The Japanese and the Chinese before them have enjoyed tofu for several thousands of years. Indeed, there is a temple in Japan which bears a long inscription extolling tofu's virtues. "Religious faith should be like tofu; it is good under any circumstances", it begins, and concludes: "Though apparently ordinary, it is extra-ordinary".

And yes, tofu's origins are humble enough. It comes from the soybean, which is now grown all over the world. What makes it remarkable is its nutritional value. It is low in sodium and saturated fats and totally free of cholesterol. It is also, ounce for ounce, the cheapest and richest source of protein available in the world except for eggs (which are high in cholesterol). Protein is essential to build a healthy body and mind, while medical authorities are now generally agreed that a diet low in sodium and cholesterol can do a lot to offset heart disease. Moreover, tofu is one of the cheapest and most versatile food sources available.

It is obviously not for nothing that the nations of the Orient have built a vast and colourful cuisine around tofu. Their culinary repertoire includes more than five hundred tofu dishes. It is eaten cold, hot, stuffed, fried, served in soups and mixed with a variety of spicy sauces and seasonings.

But this does not mean that its use should be limited to Eastern-style food. Another good thing about tofu is its versatility. Because it has a mild taste and texture, it readily absorbs the flavours of other ingredients. For this reason Western-style cuisine can also utilize this one remarkable food.

Most of the ingredients specified here are readily available from neighbourhood supermarkets. A few may prove more difficult to find, but, where possible, alternatives are suggested. Tofu itself can be purchased in many specialty and health food stores. It comes vacuum-packed and pasteurized which gives it a refrigerated shelf life of up to six weeks. But, because really fresh tofu tastes the best, why not try preparing it at home?

Making your own tofu, here demonstrated in easy to follow step-by-step detail, is both fun and highly rewarding. All the utensils required are standard kitchen-ware – bowls, a blender, colander and straining cloth. The tofu-making process will also appeal to the thrifty, as it entails no waste whatsoever. When the cooked soybeans are strained, the protein-rich residue, which the Japanese call 'okara' is not discarded, but kept and used for main meal dishes, desserts, cakes and snacks. The soymilk can be heated to produce yuba, another tofu by-product described here, while the tofu itself can be transformed by deep-frying into 'agé'. This is delicious in a risotto, grilled, or sliced to form pouches. These can be stuffed with all sorts of delicious goodies.

Though tofu itself may be unfamiliar to you, cooking with it is a simple art. Tofu is still exotic enough to surprise and delight guests. And by following the recipes that follow, you can be sure of serving delicious, unusual and healthy fare.

ALL ABOUT TOFU

Though Tofu has been a staple of Japanese cooking for literally thousands of years, it is a relatively new food in the West. This section sets out the key tofu basics, so enabling you to realize the full potential of this wonder food when you come to the recipes that follow. You will find here everything you need to know – from buying and storing guidelines and a reliable step-by-step method for making your own tofu to ways of utilizing tofu by-products in your cooking.

The point to remember throughout is that tofu, as well as being extremely healthy, is one of the world's most versatile foods. Because it absorbs the flavours of other ingredients, it can be used in a whole range of exciting ways in a great number of dishes. So, do not feel you are limited to the recipes in this book – feel free to experiment. By doing this, you will soon come to realize just what scope tofu can offer you, whether you are making a quick snack or a full meal.

ALL ABOUT TOFU

*T*ofu, a staple food of the Orient for several thousands of years, is a newcomer to the West. It is a remarkable food, rich in protein, low in saturated fats and totally free of cholesterol. In the East, it has long been a vital source of protein; in fact a whole cuisine is centred around this basic food. Because it has a light, somewhat bland flavour, it mixes well with other ingredients, both sweet and savoury. In the recipes that follow, you will see how this nutritious food can be used in every part of the meal.

Literally translated, the name tofu means soybean curd. It is prepared by soaking and grinding the beans, boiling the resulting purée and straining it to produce soy milk. A coagulant is added to the milk to make it curdle and the curds are then spooned out and preserved. Fresh tofu tastes the best, but the processed product can now be bought at health food and specialist stores.

If you are purchasing ready-made tofu, check that it is fresh and also pasteurized as the pasteurisation gives it a longer shelf life. However, making your own tofu gives the added bonus of yielding by-products which are delicious, healthy and nutritious in their own right – okara, the soybean residue – soymilk, and yuba which is made from the skin of steaming soymilk. Recipes using all these products and agé which is made by deep-frying tofu, are all included in this book.

Recognizing that the majority of cooks will find tofu somewhat exotic and unusual, this book provides a gentle initiation to the art of using this nutritious Oriental ingredient to produce delicious Western-style fare.

WHAT IS TOFU? BUYING AND STORING GUIDELINES

*T*ofu or bean curd or 'soybean curd', has been a staple of the Oriental diet for at least two thousand years. It is a by-product of the humble soybean and is made by soaking the beans in water, grinding them to a pulp, and cooking and straining them to produce soymilk, to which a coagulant is added. This makes the milk curdle, yielding the curds which are the tofu itself.

Tofu is not only a highly nutritious food in its own right; it is also a very versatile ingredient. Because it has a light texture and flavour, it can be used as effectively in appetizers and snacks as in the main course or desserts. Rich in proteins, vitamins and minerals, it is also low in calories and saturated fats and entirely free of cholesterol. So it is an ideal slimming food.

However, it is important to purchase tofu when it is fresh, if you are buying the processed product. Although manufacturers vacuum-pack and pasteurize their tofu to give it a refrigerated shelf life of up to six weeks, it is always best to select the container with the latest date stamp. Fresh tofu is creamy white and has little or no odour. Make sure that the package is not swollen, and that the contents are not foamy.

Whether home-made or purchased, the fresher the tofu, the better it will taste. Ideally, it should be used as soon as possible, but, if you need to store it for a few days, it should be unwrapped and kept in a refrigerator in a container of water deep enough to cover the whole block. The container should be covered, so that no food odours are absorbed by the tofu and the water should be changed every day.

Treated this way the tofu should remain fresh for about a week from the day it was made. If the tofu has to be kept fresh a little longer, it can be parboiled for five minutes in water to which a little salt has been added. This will increase the life of the tofu and prevent it becoming hard and porous when cooked. However, it will change the taste slightly and thus you should be careful how you use it.

One further option is to freeze the tofu which can then be stored indefinitely. Simply drain and wrap the tofu before placing it in the freezing compartment of a refrigerator. During the freezing process, the texture of the tofu changes from creamy to chewy and meatlike: the Japanese call this kind of tofu 'koyadofu'. When you want to use it, thaw completely until soft, squeeze out the excess liquid, and crumble or cube. Add frozen tofu to your favourite stew, soup or casserole instead of the usual meat, chicken or fish.

Lastly, remember that tofu must be handled with care. As it breaks apart easily, be sure to lift it gently from the refrigerator container. One way of ensuring that the block stays whole is to invert the container holding the tofu into a large bowl filled with water. The tofu will float and can then be scooped out by hand.

MAKING YOUR OWN TOFU

An essential element of the art of tofu cooking is preparing your own tofu at home. In Japan, the home of tofu, bean curd is always used fresh, usually on the day it is made. You will gain both pleasure and a real sense of achievement from following these instructions to create your own tofu: the fresh product is always preferred by tofu connoisseurs.

Ingredients:
13½oz (370g) soybeans, washed
1½ to 1¾ teaspoons nigari (if available) or calcium sulphate (0.5 to 1% volume of soy milk)

1. Soak the soybeans overnight in a large bowl with 3 pints (1.7l) water. Rinse the beans with fresh water and drain.

2. Bring 2 pints (1.13l) of water to the boil in a large saucepan. As the water is heating, put one cup of the drained beans and 1 pint (½l) of water in a blender.

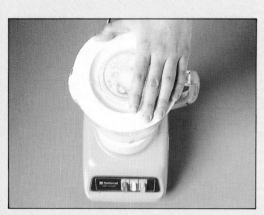

3. Seal the blender and purée the beans until smooth. Pour the puréed beans into the boiling water and turn off the heat.

4. Continue to purée the remaining drained soybeans and add them to the pan.

5. Boil the puréed soybeans (now called 'slurry') for 20 minutes. Stir from time to time to keep the slurry from burning. If the liquid begins to foam, reduce the heat and stir with a wooden spoon to break up the foam.

6. To strain the slurry, dampen a gauze cloth or clean tea towel, spread it over a colander and place the colander over a large pan. Carefully pour in the slurry.

7. Gather up the corners of the cloth to form a bag. Using the bottom of a clean jar or wooden paddle, press as much soymilk as possible from the bag.

8. When all the slurry has been strained, rinse out the cooking pot with 1 pint (½l) water. Pour through the gauze and press again. Lift the colander and gauze from the pot. Remove the soy pulp or okara from the gauze, but do not discard. Cool it, wrap and store in a refrigerator or freezer. (See last chapter for recipes that use okara as an ingredient). Rinse the gauze and set aside.

10. Stir the soymilk back and forth with a wooden spoon. Add ⅓ of the calcium sulphate or nigari solution. Stir gently and then add another ⅓ of the solution.

9. Bring the soymilk to the boil, stirring constantly. Remove from the heat. In a small bowl, mix ½ pint (¼l) water and the calcium sulphate or nigari.

11. Cover the pan and wait three minutes for curds to form. After three minutes, stir the milky portions in the pan and sprinkle these areas with the remaining solution. If there are no milky areas, proceed immediately to the next step. Otherwise, cover the pan and wait another three minutes.

12. Gently stir the surface of the pan's contents then move the spoon under the top curds to free any of the uncurdled milk that may be below. At this point, the curds should be floating in a clear, yellow liquid (whey). If not a little more calcium sulphate or nigari can be sprinkled over uncurdled areas. Cover the pot and wait for another three minutes.

13. To make rectangular blocks of tofu, perforate a wooden box, lay over the redampened gauze or cloth and strain the curds into the box.

14. Alternatively, lay the redampened cloth over the colander in the sink and spoon in the curds.

15. If using the box, when full, fold the gauze over the surface.

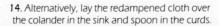

16. Cover with the lid and weight the top – a jug of water serves the purpose well.

17. If using a colander, fold the cloth over the tofu, cover with a plate and set the jug or other weight on this.

18. Drain for about fifteen minutes or longer for a firmer tofu. Remove the box or colander from the sink.

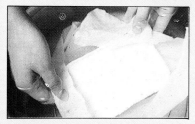

19. Fill the sink with cool water. Remove the weight and invert the tofu on a plate, using the buoyancy of the water. Remove the box or colander and gently unwrap the tofu. Allow to cool in the water for about ten minutes. Lift the tofu out of the water and keep it under refrigeration in a colander with fresh water.

20. Serve the tofu fresh with shoyu (soy) sauce or use it in one of the many recipes we provide.

OKARA AND YUBA

*T*he remarkable versatility of the soybean has been fully explored by its Oriental consumers to produce an interesting and extensive soy cuisine. Having virtually eliminated any element of waste during processing, they have developed a range of soy products from the bean itself to various fermented soybean seasonings, such as miso or soy sauce, to the bean sprouts that germinate from soaked soy beans. And of course, tofu and soy milk, which are fully described elsewhere in this book.

There are two tofu by-products which, however, deserve special mention – okara and yuba. Okara is the fibrous soybean residue which remains when the beans are boiled, crushed and strained to produce soymilk. Traditionally, the Japanese have eaten okara seasoned and cooked with vegetables. For a while, it was somewhat disparaged and so discarded, but is today enjoying a revival. And rightly so for, like so many other soy products, it is highly nutritious and imparts a pleasant nutty flavour to a variety of dishes. It is rich in protein and is also a good source of dietary fibre, which medical authorities now generally consider a useful aid in combating a whole range of diseases from diverticulosis to diabetes.

To make okara, simply follow the instructions for home-made tofu, soaking the beans, puréeing them and boiling the purée to form slurry. The Japanese themselves use the slurry, which they call 'go', as an ingredient in miso soup. For the purposes of okara and tofu-making, however, the slurry is strained and pressed. It is at this stage that okara is formed. As mentioned above, this is the soybean pulp left when the beans are strained through gauze. It should be removed carefully from the cloth, allowed to cool, wrapped and then stored.

When you cook with stored okara, you may find it a little moist and stiff. It can easily, however, be crumbled by hand and dried in several different ways. For dishes such as Okara Carrot Cake, drying can be achieved by stir-frying in an ungreased pan. If a drier, finer grained okara is required, it should be fried until it becomes light and fluffy and then sifted through a colander. Okara can also be dried by baking it in the oven. Once dry, the crumbs should be stored in an air-tight container and will keep like this at room temperature for about three weeks.

Yuba, another soybean by-product, is formed from the light yellow film on the surface of steaming soymilk. The ingenious Chinese discovered its nutritional value and introduced it to Japan where it gained wide popularity. Once limited to the cuisine of vegetarian Buddhist priests, it was produced in only moderate quantities but is now enjoying something of a revival as interest in the soy cuisine expands.

Like other soy products, yuba is very healthy. It is almost

54 per cent pure protein and just over 33 per cent fat – but fat of the polyunsaturated kind now favoured by many medical specialists.

Making yuba, described in detail on p.22 begins with heating soymilk. The film that forms on the milk as it warms is lifted off with two wooden chopsticks or bamboo sticks and then dried partly or entirely, keeping the leaves of yuba separate. The skimming process can be continued a number of times but to prolong it results in films of poor quality, low in protein and fat content.

Cooking with yuba is both rewarding and fun. The recipes in this book show how to create tasty steamed and fried yuba rolls with luscious fillings such as shrimps, chicken or nuts. And the Chinese are exploring other uses for yuba as they develop economic methods for its mass production. The latest idea is to flavour and bind together layers of yuba to resemble meat. And who knows, by the 21st century perhaps, yuba for Sunday roast may not seem such a far-fetched idea.

KITCHEN STYLE SOYMILK

Ingredients:
7½oz (212g) soybeans

R ich tasty soymilk is another gourmet treat. It is delicious freshly-made and very healthy too. This recipe makes a creamy soymilk which can be diluted or used direct for yuba (p.23) or soy whip (p.102).

Nutritionally soymilk differs little from regular cow's milk and is just as tasty. But unlike regular milk, it does have the virtue of containing vegetable oils which are low in cholesterol. All you need to make your own soymilk are the soybeans and basic kitchen utensils – a colander, a blender, a large heavy-based pan and a large loosely-woven cloth for straining. Then, simply follow the instructions below.

1. Wash the soybeans and soak them overnight in ¾ pint (426ml) water.

2. After soaking, rinse the beans, drain well and divide into two portions.

3. Dampen a cloth and use it to line a colander. Place the colander inside a pan. Stand the pan in the kitchen sink.

4. Bring a full kettle of water to the boil and keep it at a full rolling boil.

5. Pour some of the boiling water into a blender to warm it, taking care that the blender can withstand the heat. Set this aside for a few minutes. Keep the remaining water at a full boil.

6. Empty the blender jar and add one portion of the beans together with 15fl oz (426ml) boiling water. Purée for one minute. Pour the hot purée into the lined colander. Repeat the process with the second portion of beans.

7. Take the corners of the straining cloth and twist them together to form a bag. Using the base of a clean glass jar, press the soymilk from the soy pulp or okara.

8. Rinse the blender with 6fl oz (170ml) boiling water and add this to the contents of the straining cloth. Press again.

9. Cook the soymilk over a low heat for 20 minutes. Stir frequently as soymilk has a tendency to burn.

10. Cool the milk quickly by setting the pot in cold water. Change the water frequently. Pour the cooled milk into clean jars or containers. Cover and store in the refrigerator.

This recipe makes about 1 quart (2.27l) of soymilk

Do not discard the soybean residue. Okara adds a delicious nutty flavour to a variety of dishes.

HOW TO PREPARE YUBA

D elicate yuba, another protein-rich soy product, can be rolled and stuffed with a delicious variety of fillings. Making it at home requires some skill but you can easily master it if you follow the step-by-step instructions here. You will need an oblong enamel pan 5in x 19in (13cm x 23cm) or a heavy frying pan. This is used as a steaming container. By setting this in a larger pan filled with water, you can create your own double-boiler system. This, a wooden chopstick and the prepared soymilk are all that is required.

1. Pour the soymilk into the steaming container to a depth of 1-2in (2.5-5cm). Heat the soymilk until it is steaming but not boiling. Wait for a skin to form on the surface (about 7-10 minutes). Using a knife cut the skin free from the edges of the pan. Premoisten a chopstick and slip it under the skin.

2. Carefully lift off the skin or yuba, taking care not to let the sheet tear. Allow it to drain on the chopstick for a few moments.

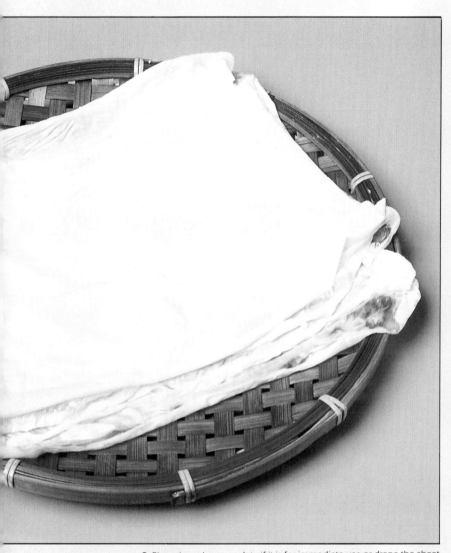

3. Place the yuba on a plate if it is for immediate use or drape the sheet over a moistened bamboo basket to dry. Repeat the process while the skin remains strong. This recipe should make around 15 sheets.

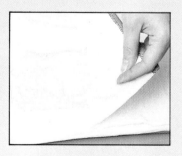

4. To store yuba, wrap it loosely in plastic wrap and keep it in the refrigerator. It can also be frozen or air-dried until brittle. To reconstitute, moisten two dish cloths, wring out the excess moisture and spread one cloth on a clean surface. Dip a sheet of yuba in a bowl of cold water for a few moments.

5. Place it on the cloth. Dip the other dried sheets one by one and lay them out too. Cover all the yuba sheets with the second moist cloth and allow to stand until the yuba is pliable.

AGE

PREPARING AGE

Another popular way of using tofu is to deep-fry it, producing what the Japanese call agé. The tofu is cooked until golden brown in colour and served, cut in strips or squares, in soups and risottos. Alternatively squares of agé can be slit to form pouches and stuffed with a variety of luscious savoury fillings.

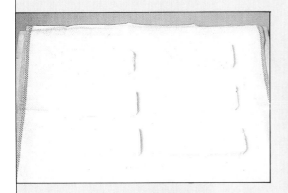

1. Cut the tofu into slices about ⅓in (8mm) thick and lay out on a dry cloth.
2. Cover the slices with another cloth and allow to stand for 20 minutes.

3. Change the cloths and weight with a flat board and a bowl of water to extract as much moisture as possible from the tofu.

4. Using a large frying pan, pour in enough vegetable oil mixed with sesame oil, to deep-fry the slices. The sesame oil imparts a nut-like flavour. Heat the oil to a temperature of 356°F (180°C). Slowly deep-fry the slices until golden in colour, taking care that they remain immersed in oil during cooking. When cooked, remove from the pan and drain well. When all the slices are cooked, reheat the oil to 446°F (230°C) and quickly re-fry the slices. The second stage of frying dries the surface of the tofu and fixes its shape.

AGE POUCHES

1. Place a slice of agé on a clean surface and pat lightly with a rolling pin.

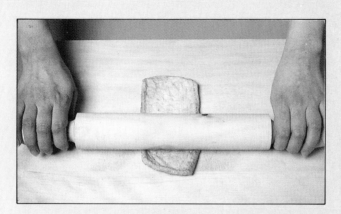
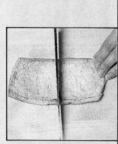

2. Using a sharp knife, cut the slice in half, cross-wise.

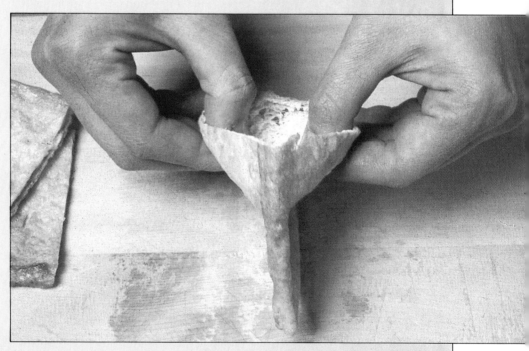

3. Gently pull the edges apart to form a pouch and wash out with water to remove excess oil

*B*efore attempting to cook with tofu, it is best to learn the basic tofu preparation techniques – steaming, scrambling, pressing, puréeing or blending, parboiling and draining. All six methods are described below.

STEAMING

Steaming heats the tofu quickly without impairing its vitamin and mineral content. And, because this method involves no additional cooking fat or oils, it is an ideal way to prepare a slimming meal.

Method: To steam, you do not have to possess a steamer. Almost any saucepan can be adapted by placing a trivet – a small tripod – over the base to keep the tofu above the level of the water in the pan

You can make your own trivet by removing the top and bottom of a can and then resting a heat-proof plate on it. For the correct steaming time, the specific recipe must be followed.

SCRAMBLING

Scrambling causes the tofu to give off liquid whey. After scrambling, the tofu will resemble the texture of cottage cheese and be slightly firm.

Method: Place the tofu in a saucepan or frying pan. Sprinkle with salt to taste. Cook over a medium heat, stirring with a wooden spoon to break up the tofu into small pieces. After about five minutes, the tofu will resemble cottage cheese and the whey will separate from the curds. Next, line a colander with a cloth and pour the separated tofu through this to drain off the whey. To extract as much moisture as possible, gather up the corners of the cloth to form a sack and twist to expel the whey. Allow the scrambled tofu to cool at room temperature.

PRESSING

Tofu is pressed to expel the moisture. This causes the tofu to become firm while preserving its shape.

Method: Two different methods are used in this book – the 'towel and refrigerator' method and the 'pressing' method.

For the first, wrap the tofu in a folded cotton tea towel and set on a plate in the refrigerator for the time specified in the recipe.

For the pressing method, wrap the tofu in a folded tea towel and place on a flat board or plate next to the sink.

Raise one end of the board about half an inch, to allow the tofu to drain. Place a board and a 2lb ((0.9kg) weight over the wrapped tofu and allow to stand for 15 minutes or as the recipe directs.

PUREEING OR BLENDING

This is one of the most popular ways of preparing tofu. Blending renders tofu creamy and smooth making it suitable for a wide variety of dips, spreads, soups, sauces, dressings and desserts.

Method: For easy blending, first pour the liquid ingredients into the blender. Add the tofu little by little so as not to overwork the blender's motor. Tofu can be blended alone by puréeing the tofu a little at a time, stopping occasionally to scrape the puréed tofu to the centre of the blender.

PARBOILING

Parboiling tofu serves a variety of purposes. It warms the tofu, freshens stored tofu that might show signs of spoiling, firms up the tofu and adds taste if parboiled in a flavoured broth or salted water.

Method: Boil water in a saucepan. Add the tofu, reduce the heat and cover. Continue heating for a few minutes or until the tofu is warmed.

DRAINING

Draining helps keep the tofu firm and preserves its natural sweetness which can be lost if it is immersed in water. This method is used when tofu is to be cooked in a flavoured broth.

Method: Place the tofu in a colander over a bowl or container. Cover and place in the refrigerator for one tc two hours or as the recipe directs.

Appetizers and Snacks
Tofu Party Canapés * Artichoke Hearts With Tofu Sesame Sauce * Fruit Shake * Man's Cake * Whole Wheat Cheese rolls * Easy Tofu Liver Spread * Trout Spread * Tofu Mushroom Terrine

APPETIZERS AND SNACKS

All cooks like to surprise and entertain guests, so it always pays to have something special and tasty to hand. There are several criteria such food should fulfill. It has to be colourful and delicious. And it is an added bonus if it is healthy too. The recipes here meet all these demands. A dish such as Tofu Party Canapés can be a spectacular mixture of creamy white tofu and colourful fresh vegetables, while Man's Cake is an eye-catching artistic and nutritious creation. While it takes a little time and patience to make Tofu Mushroom Terrine, the results well repay the effort.

Tofu Liver Spread and Tofu Trout Spread are both delicious. Tofu adds protein and absorbs the flavour of sesame in a tasty recipe for Artichoke Hearts With Tofu, and combines equally well with cheese when it comes to making Whole Wheat Cheese Rolls. And there is one treat to share or enjoy on your own – luscious Fruit Shake, a healthy confection of milk, fruit and nutritious tofu.

TOFU PARTY CANAPES

1¼lb (600g) tofu, pressed
Flour for dredging
Salt and white pepper
Salad oil for frying

For garnish:

Cheese, caviar, chicken slices,
cottage cheese, tomato slices,
anchovies, tuna flakes, fried
bacon, minced chives, boiled
shrimps etc.

Tofu, served hot or cold, is an excellent basis for party food. It adds nutrition but not bulk to snacks and its light, pleasant taste will enhance the flavour of the colourful garnishes used. With a little imagination, Tofu Party Canapés will prove a pièce de résistance at any festive occasion.

To prepare hot canapés, cut the tofu into slices about 1 x 2in (2.5 x 5cm) and ¼in (7mm) thick. Sprinkle with salt and pepper. Dredge the tofu with flour and fry the slices on each side until crisp and brown. Arrange the grilled tofu on a warmed plate. Decorate with the garnishes of choice and serve warm.

For cold canapés, spread the tofu slices on a cloth. Sprinkle with one tablespoonful of salt and allow to stand for 30 minutes. Decorate with garnishes such as fresh fruit, avocado slices or marinated fish and keep cool until ready to serve.

ARTICHOKE HEARTS WITH TOFU SESAME SAUCE

16 artichoke hearts (canned or
freshly boiled), drained
6oz (170g) mashed tofu
3 tablespoons ground sesame
seeds

1 teaspoon salt
½ teaspoon sugar
1 tablespoon sesame oil
2 tablespoons lemon juice or
cider vinegar

This tofu dish with its distinctive sesame flavour, makes an unusual and delicious hors d'oeuvre or accompaniment to a cold salad meal. Its added bonus is that it is both quick and easy to prepare.

First squeeze the tofu to remove excess moisture. Place in a blender with all the other ingredients, except the artichoke hearts. Blend until smooth. Stop the machine from time to time to scrape the blender bowl with a rubber spatula, removing any of the mixture that has adhered to the sides. Cut the artichoke hearts into chunks. Mix with the sauce and serve.

A more substantial sauce is obtained by adding three hard-boiled egg yolks to the sauce which can then be piped decoratively over the artichokes.

FRUIT SHAKE

¼ pint (0.14l) cold milk
2½oz (70g) mashed tofu
5oz (142g) chopped fruit
(banana, peaches,
strawberries etc.)

1 tablespoon sugar (or to taste)
⅛ teaspoon salt
2 to 3 drops vanilla essence
2-4 ice cubes

For a luscious and highly nutritious fruit shake, simply put all the ingredients in a blender. Mix until smooth. Pour into a large glass. And enjoy!

Party treat These colourful canapés will enhance the atmosphere of any party. Make them a table centrepiece.

MAN'S CAKE

2lb (850g) tofu
A: 2 tablespoons paprika
5-6 drops tabasco
½ teaspoon salt
¼ teaspoon pepper
4 tablespoons tomato paste
1 tablespoon very finely minced
   onion

B: ¼ teaspoon pepper
2 tablespoons very finely
   chopped chives
2 tablespoons very finely
   chopped parsley and other
   herbs of your choice (tarragon,
   chervil, borage, mint, etc.)

C: ½ teaspoon salt
¼ teaspoon pepper
2 tablespoons finely chopped
   onion
2 teaspoons hot mustard
2 hard-boiled eggs, finely
   chopped
2 tablespoons mayonnaise

For shortcrust:
14oz (396g) flour
7oz (198g) butter
1 small egg
A pinch of salt
3 tablespoons cold water

The stunning appearance of this eye-catching party piece is only surpassed by the taste – deliciously different savoury fillings layered together between delicate rounds of short-crust pastry.

First prepare the shortcrust pastry (see p.103) and then set aside for two hours in the refrigerator. Divide the dough into three equal portions. Roll one portion out into a circle about ⅕in (5mm) thick. Place a plate 10in (25cm) in diameter over it and trim round the edge with a knife to remove the surplus pastry. Preheat the oven to 400°F (200°C). Roll out the other portions of dough to form three rounds, also 10in (25cm) in diameter. Cook the four rounds on greased baking trays until crisp, keeping the first round separate as this thicker portion forms the base of the cake. To prepare the filling, crumble the tofu into a saucepan, add two teaspoons of salt and cook for three minutes. Drain and wrap in a large cloth. Press to expel the moisture. Then divide the tofu into three equal portions. Assemble the ingredients A and mix with one portion of the tofu. Spread the mixture over the first thicker round of pastry. Mix the second tofu portion with ingredients B and spread this on the second round of pastry. Repeat the process with ingredients C, spreading the mixture on the third pastry round. Sandwich the layers together, topping with the

Man's cake This attractive dish tastes as good as it looks. The savoury fillings sandwiched between the pastry layers all add to its savour.

fourth pastry round. The garnish lends the final artistic touch. Arrange alfalfa sprouts over the surface and circles of sliced radishes and shredded carrot over the centre. As an appetizer, Man's Cake is then ready to serve. However, if you wish to make it the centrepiece of a more substantial meal, a mixed lettuce salad is an excellent accompaniment.

WHOLE WHEAT CHEESE ROLLS

Crunchy croissants Tofu and Parmesan cheese combine to make these deliciously healthy croissants a man-sized snack.

1lb (453g) tofu
4oz (113g) butter or margarine
1oz (28g) grated Parmesan
   cheese
1 teaspoon salt

8½oz (240g) whole wheat flour
2 teaspoons baking powder
1 teaspoon oregano (optional)
1oz (28g) grated Parmesan
   cheese for rolling dough

To prepare these healthy and nutritious croissant rolls, combine the tofu, butter, 4oz Parmesan cheese and salt in a blender until smooth. Set aside. In a large bowl, mix together the whole wheat flour, baking powder and oregano. Add the tofu to form a soft, sticky dough. Divide the dough into two equal portions. Sprinkle a sheet of wax paper with two tablespoons Parmesan cheese. Place one portion of dough over the cheese, sprinkling the top with a little flour to prevent it sticking to your fingers. Flatten the dough to to form a round about ½in (12mm) thick. Cut the dough into eight equal triangular segments. Roll each segment from its widest end to the tip and curve to form a crescent shape. Repeat with the other half of the dough.

Preheat an oven to 375°F (180°C) and bake for about 30 minutes or until the rolls are firm to the touch.

EASY TOFU LIVER SPREAD

10oz (283g) tofu
4 tablespoons minced onion
10oz (283g) pork liver
8oz (226g) minced meat (beef,
    pork or chicken)
3 tablespoons salad oil
1 chicken or beef stock cube
½ teaspoon salt

¼ teaspoon black pepper
1 tablespoon oregano
1 tablespoon sweet thyme or
    fine herbs
4 tablespoons brandy
2 tablespoons cornflour
4-8 tablespoons of double
    cream (optional)

Tasty tofu liver spread which is particularly rich in both protein and iron is an interesting and economical hors d'oeuvre or sandwich filling. This recipe makes about four cups of spread which can be kept for up to a week in a refrigerator or two months in a deep-freeze.

To prepare, wrap the tofu in a cloth and allow to stand for 15 minutes to expel moisture. Clean the liver well under cold water and pat dry. Sauté the onion in oil for a few minutes, add the liver and minced meat and fry until well-browned. Add the tofu, seasoning and spices and bring to the boil, stirring from time to time. Pour the brandy over the mixture, light it and wait until the flame has died. Sprinkle cornflour over the mixture and cook for another three minutes, stirring constantly. Cover the pan and cook the mixture for a few minutes. Then remove the lid and cook over a medium heat until the liquid is reduced by one half. Set the pan aside for 15 minutes to cool. Pour the mixture into a blender and mix until the desired texture is achieved. For a lighter colour and thinner consistency, add the heavy cream. Turn out the mixture into little ramekins or a medium-sized earthenware dish and store in the refrigerator until required.

TROUT SPREAD

10oz (283g) tofu
3 fillets of smoked trout (5-6oz,
    150-180g)
4 tablespoons salad oil
3 tablespoons cider vinegar
1 teaspoon hot mustard

½ teaspoon salt
⅛ teaspoon pepper
3 tablespoons chopped capers,
    minced pickles or minced
    onion as garnish

Smoked trout is delicious in the tofu spread but the recipe readily permits variations if other smoked fish such as mackerel are preferred.

Commence preparation by crumbling the tofu in a saucepan and cooking over a high heat for two minutes, stirring constantly. Remove from the heat immediately if the tofu becomes dry or yellowish in colour. Press the tofu in a cloth to expel the moisture.

Combine all the ingredients, including the tofu, in a blender and mix to the desired consistency.

Serve the spread accompanied by the chopped capers, pickles and onion, as an hors d'oeuvres with thin slices of toast or as a sandwich filling on crusty bread.

Picnic or supper-time specials
Tofu spreads like Liver and Trout, complemented by crudités and fresh crusty bread, make tasty, healthy snacks.

TOFU MUSHROOM TERRINE

9oz (255g) veal
½ teaspoon salt
⅛ teaspoon pepper
1 teaspoon paprika powder
17½oz (500g) tofu
26oz (750g) fresh mushrooms
   or 17oz (480g) net weight
   canned mushrooms, drained
4oz (113g) pork fat, cut into
   small pieces (optional)

3 tablespoons salad oil
8 tablespoons minced shallot or
   onion
4 tablespoons brandy
2oz (56g) breadcrumbs
8 tablespoons double cream
9oz (255g) bacon, or enough to
   cover the whole terrine
3 sticks crabmeat

Complex as the preparation for this dish may appear, it is an exercise that well repays the effort, both in terms of taste and appearance.

First, remove all pieces of tough meat from the veal and cut the remainder into small pieces, seasoning with salt, pepper and paprika. Set aside. Wrap the tofu in a large cloth and press for 15 minutes. Meanwhile, clean and wash the mushrooms under cold running water. Drain them in a colander. In a frying pan, heat the oil and sauté the onion and mushrooms for five minutes. Add the brandy and bring to the boil. Drain and allow to cool.

To make the stuffing, combine all the ingredients, except the mushrooms and bacon, in a blender and mix until smooth. Fill the terrine in layers by first lining the base and walls with the bacon. Use one third of the stuffing for the first layer. Spread half of the mushroom mixture over

Line the base and the walls of the tin with bacon.

Spread half of the mushroom mixture evenly over the stuffing.

Use one third of the stuffing mixture to make the first layer.

this, distributing it evenly. Repeat with the next third of the mixture, placing the crabmeat or other colourful ingredients in the centre as a decoration. Fill the terrine with the final third of the stuffing, smoothing over the surface with a spatula. Cover tightly with bacon slices.

A gourmet delight Attractive and tasty Tofu Mushroom Terrine is sure to bring compliments to the chef.

To cook, preheat the oven to 325°F (160°C). Fill a shallow pan to ⅓ its height with water. Place the terrine in the pan and bake covered for 45 minutes. When properly cooked, the centre should spring back to the touch. Take out of the oven and allow to stand for at least two hours to set.

Finally, heat a French loaf, garlic bread or crusty rolls and serve hot with slices of the cooled terrine.

Use another third of the stuffing to form the next layer with colourful ingredients in the centre for decoration. Then fill the tin with the final third.

Cover tightly with bacon slices. Place tin in the pan.

Tofu Sauces And Party Dips
Spinach Dip * Tofu Blue Cheese Dip * Curry Dip * Tofu Tuna Dip * Tofu Mushroom Dip * Party Dip * Tofu White Sauce * All Purpose Tofu Sauce * Herb Dressing * Tofu Cottage Cheese * Tofu Mayonnaise * Tofu Cream Cheese * Creamed Tofu

TOFU SAUCES AND PARTY DIPS

Party dips and sauces are fun to create but often entail hours of labour and rich ingredients which spell disaster for the figure-conscious. Here, we try to avoid those pitfalls.

Tofu is the base for a delicious array of both dips and sauces, not to mention the sauces that can be used as dips and vice versa. Its great advantage is that it blends well and absorbs a variety of flavours. Using tofu, in many cases, eliminates the need for a creamy or starchy ingredient to thicken the mixture. This is a double bonus. Because tofu has so few calories, tofu-based sauces and dips are a boon to dieters. Because tofu is rich in protein, they are also highly nutritious and combined with a vegetable provide a substantial snack or even meal.

SPINACH DIP

8oz (226g) mashed tofu
¼ teaspoon dry mustard
½ teaspoon salt
3 tablespoons cider vinegar
8 tablespoons salad oil
8 tablespoons chopped parsley

2½oz (71g) chopped spring
  onions
1 10oz (283g) package frozen
  spinach, thawed, squeezed
  and coarsely chopped

To prepare this quick, attractive dip, mix the tofu, mustard, salt, vinegar and oil in a blender until smooth. Pour the blended mixture into a bowl and stir in the remaining ingredients.

To make this dip into a spectacular party centrepiece, hollow out a large round crusty loaf and fill it with the mixture.

Serve immediately or after refrigeration, with cubes of bread hollowed out from the loaf, plus crackers and a selection of crisp, fresh vegetables.

Tasty and healthy party food
A colourful array of delicious tofu dips complemented by fresh bread and vegetable sticks.

TOFU BLUE CHEESE DIP

10oz (283g) tofu
4oz (113g) blue cheese
8 tablespoons sour cream

½ teaspoon salt
¼ teaspoon pepper

This is a tangy party dip, sure to tempt your guests.

To prepare it, first take the tofu, wrap it in a cloth and leave it to stand for 20 minutes at room temperature. Then, place it in a blender with the rest of the ingredients and purée the mixture to a very smooth consistency.

Serve the dip with vegetable sticks, cut from cucumber, carrot and celery. The natural flavour of the vegetables will be complemented by the taste of the tofu.

The dip can be kept, chilled in the refrigerator, for two to three days.

CURRY DIP

½ teaspoon dry mustard
1½ teaspoons curry powder
½ teaspoon cider vinegar

4¼oz (120g) Tofu Mayonnaise
  (p.46)
1½ teaspoons honey

This dip, which is quick and easy to prepare, captures the genuine taste of the Orient.

Simply measure out the ingredients and purée them in a blender until smooth. To accentuate the distinctive flavour, serve the dip chilled.

Crisp slices of carrot, cucumber or celery make excellent dip sticks. As a tangy alternative, try serving the dip with fresh fruit.

TOFU TUNA DIP

10oz (283g) tofu
1 can (about 160g solid weight)
  flaked tuna, drained
3 tablespoons minced onion
2 teaspoons hot mustard

2 teaspoons paprika
5-6 drops tabasco
3 tablespoons lemon juice
1 tablespoon fine herbs

To prepare this healthy protein-rich dip, take the tofu and set it aside, wrapped in a cloth for 15 minutes. Next, place the tofu in a blender and mix until smooth, adding all the remaining ingredients – except the salt and pepper – just before the blending is completed. Season with salt and pepper according to taste.

For a fuller fishier flavour, the amount of tuna can be increased. Serve the dip with bread, crackers or a selection of fresh vegetables.

SAUCES AND DIPS

TOFU MUSHROOM DIP

10oz (283g) tofu
2 tablespoons minced onion
8 tablespoons double cream
1 chicken stock cube, dissolved
   in 4 tablespoons boiling water

½ teaspoon pepper
7oz (198g) fresh mushrooms
   wiped clean and stemmed
1 tablespoon butter
½ teaspoon salt

To prepare this delicious creamy dip, first wrap the tofu in a cloth, set it aside, and leave it to stand for 20 minutes. Meanwhile, measure the other ingredients and mince the onion and mushrooms, keeping the two separate.

Mix the tofu in a blender to a smooth consistency. Add the onion, cream, pepper and stock and then purée again. Fry the minced mushrooms in butter until they are soft. Add salt to taste and stir the mushrooms into the tofu mixture.

Florets of cauliflower and sticks of crisp carrots, cucumber, peppers or celery are all colourful and nutritious accompaniments. Alternatively, you could spread the dip on to slices of granary bread as a tasty sandwich treat.

PARTY DIP

3oz (85g) cream cheese
8oz (226g) mashed tofu
1¾ pints (175ml) yoghurt
½ teaspoon salt
1 tablespoon chopped parsley
1 tablespoon minced onion

To prepare this quick, tasty dip, take the cheese, tofu, yoghurt and salt and mix in a blender until smooth. Chop the parsley, mince the onion and stir them both into the mixture by hand. The dip is then ready to serve.

Fresh vegetables such as carrot sticks, florets of cauliflower and sticks of celery make an excellent accompaniment.

And, if you are looking for something really different, make the dip an artistic and culinary centrepiece by serving it in scooped out avocado halves, surrounded by the vegetables and crackers as well.

TOFU WHITE SAUCE

5.9fl oz (160ml) milk
10oz (283g) tofu
½ teaspoon salt
¼ teaspoon dry mustard
¼ teaspoon paprika
A pinch of freshly ground pepper
1 tablespoon butter or
    margarine (optional)

This protein-rich alternative to regular white sauce is a boon to dieters; it is also simple and quick to prepare. Combine all the ingredients together in a blender until smooth. Then pour the mixture into a saucepan and heat gently, taking care not to let it boil as this will curdle the sauce. Should the mixture separate, however, return it to the blender and mix again until a smooth consistency is achieved. This nutritious sauce is excellent poured over steamed vegetables or fish.

To make a cheese sauce, follow the above recipe but omit the butter, halve the amount of salt and add 1½ cups (200g) shredded cheddar cheese. The cheese sauce makes a tasty topping for pasta or steamed vegetables. And there is no need to worry about leftovers. Any sauce remaining can be refrigerated which gives it a firmer texture and transforms it into a deliciously different sandwich spread or a special party treat to be served on crackers and celery sticks.

Rich creamy sauces Served with vegetables or spaghetti, they are both tasty and add protein to the meal.

ALL PURPOSE TOFU SAUCE

10oz (283g) tofu
3 tablespoons ground sesame
    seeds
8 tablespoons single cream
1 tablespoon miso (soybean
    paste)
2 teaspoons salt
¼ teaspoon pepper
3 tablespoons tomato ketchup
4 tablespoons brandy
3 tablespoons salad oil
8 tablespoons chicken stock

This is a delicious and versatile sauce which is quickly and easily prepared.

First set aside the tofu, wrapped in a cloth, for 15 minutes. While it stands, assemble all the other ingredients. Measure out the stock, using fresh liquid from a stewed chicken carcass or a stock cube, and pour it into a blender. Add the remaining ingredients, including the tofu, and blend until the mixture is very smooth.

As the name suggests, this tasty tofu mix goes well with a wide variety of dishes. Heated, it makes a novel sauce to pour over spaghetti or cooked vegetables. Served cold, it becomes a spicy dressing for salads and cold meats.

For a subtle change of flavour, ½ cup of ground walnuts can be substituted for the sesame seeds.

Tofu Cottage Cheese As well as being ideally healthy accompaniments to summer dishes, tasty Tofu Herb Dressing and Cottage Cheese and Tofu Mayonnaise have their own particular flavours.

HERB DRESSING

12 tablespoons Tofu
  Mayonnaise (see below)
12 tablespoons yoghurt
8oz (226g) mashed tofu
½ teaspoon minced fresh dill
½ teaspoon salt
⅛ teaspoon pepper
1 tablespoon minced parsley
1 tablespoon minced onion

To create this deliciously fresh-tasting dressing, combine the prepared mayonnaise, yoghurt, tofu, dill, salt and pepper in a blender and mix until smooth. Stir in the parsley and onion by hand and chill until serving time.

As a dressing, this adds protein and piquancy to any salad. As a dip, it is delicious served with a variety of crisp vegetables such as sliced cucumber, peppers and carrots or florets of cauliflower.

TOFU COTTAGE CHEESE

8¾oz (250g) drained and
  pressed tofu
½ teaspoon salt

2-3 tablespoons yoghurt or sour
  cream

For a quick protein-rich cottage cheese look-alike, use a fork to mix the ingredients together until the desired consistency is achieved. For a touch of colour and a subtle variation in flavour, add chopped chives or tiny pineapple pieces. Chill before serving with basic salads or as a dip accompanied by crisp fresh vegetables. And for a really spectacular party treat, present the tofu mixture in a fresh pineapple shell.

TOFU MAYONNAISE

7oz (198g) mashed tofu
8 tablespoons salad oil
3 tablespoons cider vinegar

¼ teaspoon dry mustard
½ teaspoon salt

For a basic mayonnaise which, once refrigerated, will keep for at least a fortnight, combine all the ingredients in a blender and mix until smooth. Use immediately or cover, cool and store. The mayonnaise is an excellent accompaniment to any salad ; and can also be combined with other ingredients to make a more exotic dressing or dip.

TOFU CREAM CHEESE

Ingredients:
10oz (283g) drained and pressed tofu
2 tablespoons salad oil
¼ teaspoon salt (or to taste)

To create a cream cheese which even the most dedicated dieter can sample with a free conscience, combine all the ingredients in a blender and mix until smooth. The drained and pressed tofu may make the mixture a little too stiff and if this is the case, stop the blender and use a spatula to push the ingredients towards the centre of the machine and blend again.

The creamy tofu mix, best served chilled, makes a nutritious sandwich filling or a party special, spread on crackers or sticks of celery.

CREAMED TOFU

1¾oz (50g) butter or margarine
1 medium onion, diced
5oz (141g) sliced mushrooms
¼ teaspoon thyme
½ teaspoon salt
⅛ teaspoon pepper
4 tablespoons of white wine
5oz (141g) frozen green peas
1 clove garlic, minced
¾ pint (375ml) milk
1 tablespoon minced parsley
4 tablespoons flour
10oz (283g) cubed tofu (cut tofu into ¾in (19mm) cubes)

This delicious and versatile sauce makes a luscious pancake filling and is guaranteed to transform rice, a pastry base or just plain toast into a tasty snack or even a main meal.

To prepare it, heat the butter gently in a pan and then sauté the onion, mushroom and garlic until transparent. Add the flour, stirring the mixture constantly, pour in the milk and cook over a low heat until the sauce is thick and creamy. Add the parsley, thyme, salt, pepper and wine and lastly stir in the peas and tofu cubes. Cook until heated through and serve immediately.

This amount should serve three people.

Tofu Soup Specialities
Cream of Tofu Soup * Tofu Pumpkin Soup * Tofu in Hot
Soup, Korean Style * Tofu Custard With Asparagus Tips *
Tofu Hot Pot

TOFU SOUP SPECIALITIES

We all have our own familiar memories of soup. For many it is a childhood recollection of a warm welcoming aroma on cold winter nights. Today, alas, soup too often means fast-food – something out of a can or a packet. What has been lost along with the memory, is the element of good nutrition that came from the meaty stocks of by-gone days.

Time, or rather, the lack of it, is the most often cited excuse. But, using tofu as a basic ingredient, good protein-rich soups can be prepared quickly and easily. The recipes that follow entail the minimum of preparation. The tofu is quickly blended or cooked with other ingredients to produce rich, satisfying soups that make excellent starter dishes or can form the basis of a well-balanced main meal.

Mild and refreshing The inclusion of protein-rich tofu ensures that both Cream of Tofu Soup and Tofu Pumpkin Soup are as wholesome as they are delicious.

CREAM OF TOFU SOUP

8¾oz (250g) tofu
1 teaspoon salt
¾ pint (⅜l) milk
2 chicken stock cubes

2 tablespoons cornflour
8 tablespoons double cream
Chopped chives as garnish

For a mild, refreshing soup – a perfect starter to any meal – combine the tofu with the salt in a blender until smooth. Pour the milk into a saucepan, bring to the boil and then crumble in the stock cubes and stir gently until they are fully dissolved. Dissolve the cornflour in a little cold water and add this to the milk and stock mixture.

Cook for two minutes, stirring constantly until thickened, and then add the double cream and tofu purée. Cook until warm, taking care not to boil the mixture as this will cause the cream to curdle.

Serve the soup in small bowls, garnished with chives and accompanied by hot, crusty bread.

TOFU PUMPKIN SOUP

17½oz (500g) pumpkin
  (or winter squash)
10oz (283g) tofu
1 chicken stock cube
16 tablespoons water

¾ pint (0.42l) cold milk
2 tablespoons cornflour
1 teaspoon salt
Chopped chives as a garnish

This soup has a delicate flavour which makes it an excellent light starter to a meal.

To prepare, peel the pumpkin, using a sharp knife, discard the seeds and slice thinly. Dissolve the stock cube in boiling water in a saucepan, add the pumpkin and cook until tender. Strain the pumpkin and mix it with the tofu in a blender until a smooth consistency is achieved. Pour the milk into a saucepan and bring to the boil. Add the cornflour, dissolved in a little cold water and cook until thickened, stirring all the time. Pour in the tofu-pumpkin purée and mix until smooth. Bring the soup back to the boil and season with the salt. Pour the soup into bowls and garnish with chives.

When pumpkin is not available, substitute green peas, cooked white beans, carrots or potatoes and create your own year-round special tofu soup.

TOFU IN HOT SOUP, KOREAN STYLE

17½oz (500g) tofu
17½oz (500g) kimchi of
  Chinese cabbage (hot spicy
  vegetable preparation
  obtainable canned from
  speciality stores)
3 tablespoons shoyu (soy sauce)

1 clove of garlic, grated
½ pint (0.28l) soup stock (fresh
  or prepared from a chicken
  stock cube)
½ teaspoon sugar
1 tablespoon sesame oil
1 tablespoon chilli powder

This is a deliciously fiery, oriental soup, which is also very quick to prepare. First, cut the tofu and cabbage into bite-sized pieces and set aside. Combine the remaining ingredients in a saucepan and bring to the boil. Add the tofu and cabbage, cook for five minutes, season to taste and the soup is ready to serve.

TOFU CUSTARD WITH ASPARAGUS TIPS

10oz (283g) tofu
4 egg whites
About 30 tips and parts of
    canned white asparagus,
    drained (reserve liquid)
16 tablespoons milk
½ teaspoon salt

For the centre decoration
4 egg yolks and 1 whole egg

¼ teaspoon salt
Pepper to taste
2 tablespoons vegetable oil
5 stalks green asparagus

For the sauce
16 tablespoons liquid from the
    canned asparagus
½ chicken stock cube
1 tablespoon cornflour

This dramatic tofu dish makes an exotic and unusual alternative to soup.

Start preparation by placing the tofu in a blender and mixing until smooth. Turn the egg whites into a bowl and gently stir with a fork. Add the tofu purée, milk and salt, mix gently and set aside. Line the base of a deep serving bowl with the white asparagus and strain the tofu mixture over this.

The next step involves steaming. If you do not have a conventional steamer, improvise by using any deep saucepan with a tight-fitting lid and placing a baking rack, colander or any metal ring inside it. The idea is to raise the bowl off the saucepan's base. Make sure the water in the steamer is boiling, reduce the heat and set the bowl of asparagus and tofu mixture in the pan. Steam for 12-15 minutes.

While the tofu is steaming, scramble the eggs by beating the yolks and whole egg with salt and pepper to taste and frying in oil, taking care not to overcook. Set this aside for the garnish. The green asparagus which also serves as garnish should now be cut and fried gently in oil – to preserve the colour and crispness of the asparagus, keep the amount of oil used down to the bare minimum. Sprinkle the cooked asparagus with a pinch of salt and set aside.

For the sauce, pour the liquid from the drained white asparagus into a saucepan, crumble in the stock cube and stir until dissolved. If necessary, correct the seasoning at this stage before adding the cornflour, dissolved in cold water, to the sauce. Cook for another minute, stirring constantly, until the sauce has thickened.

By this stage, the steaming process should be complete. Remove the bowl of asparagus and tofu, which should now resemble a custard, and pour the sauce over it. Arrange the garnish of scrambled eggs, topped with the green asparagus as a centrepiece to complete this spectacular starter. Hot crusty bread is an excellent accompaniment, particularly if it is to be served as a light lunch rather than an appetizer.

TOFU HOT POT

10oz (300g) tofu
1 medium-sized onion
1 carrot
1 stalk of celery
2-3 cabbage leaves

4 small turnips
Soup stock or stock cube
Salt and pepper
4 eggs

This is a substantial, nutritious soup, full of healthy vegetables and protein-rich tofu – ideal for a cold wintry day.

To prepare clean and peel the vegetables and chop into bite-sized pieces. Boil the soup stock and add the onion, carrot and celery followed by the cabbage and turnips making sure that they all remain crisp. Season to taste with salt and pepper. Cut the tofu into bite-sized pieces and add to the other vegetables in the pan, heating gently until the tofu is warm. Break the eggs carefully into the soup mixture and when the white is set, this colourful dish is complete. Spoon into individual bowls and serve hot with buttery garlic toast.

A wholesome, hearty soup
Tasty Tofu Hot Pot is substantial enough to serve as a main course.

Custard surprise
Tofu Custard with Asparagus Tips is a delicious dish to serve on a special occasion.

The heart of the meal

Tofu Chicken Patties * Stuffed Marrow * Tofu Gratin With Eggplant * Lasagne * Tofu Chicken Dumplings * Pork Pie With Tofu Mousse * Broiled Tofu With Miso Sauce * Vegetarian Quiche * Tofu Knishes * Baked Fish With Tofu White Sauce * Fried Tofu With Green Onion * Tofu With Meat Sauce * Fine Chicken Fricassée With Tofu * Tofu Marrow Dumplings * Steamed Tofu Sandwich * Tofu Crabmeat Gratin * Vegetable Soufflé * Tofu Burgers * Italian Tofu * Deep-fried Tofu Sandwich * Chicken With Curry Stuffing * Tofu Flambé * Tuna Salad In Tomato Aspic Ring * Cooked Salad With Tofu * Tofu Wakamé * Chilled Tofu With Green Sauce * Devilled Tofu Salad * Tofu Seafood Salad

THE HEART OF THE MEAL

O nce upon a time, meat was a vital component of the main meal of the day. Our grandparents and their parents before them fervently believed that a meal without meat was a meal without true nourishment. In more recent years, of course, an enlightened view of nutrition has prompted many culinary innovations. Now we think more in terms of protein and vitamins when choosing our foods.

This approach opens up an almost limitless range of nutritional possibilities – and few as innovative as the recipes that follow. The recipes in this chapter show you how to create hearty main meals that combine taste, nourishment and variety, mixing protein-rich tofu with chicken, fish, meat and vegetables. They also show how to prepare spectacular salad dishes. Because these, too, contain tofu combined with a variety of crisp, colourful vegetables, they can serve equally as a wholesome party dish or a nutritious main meal.

TOFU CHICKEN PATTIES

10oz (283g) tofu
10oz (283g) ground chicken
  meat
12 leaves of shiso (Japanese
  mint) or nori (Japanese
  seaweed)

3 tablespoons cornflour
Salt and pepper
Vegetable oil for frying
2 tablespoons grated ginger root
2 tablespoons mustard
Flour for dredging

Tofu Chicken Patties These make a delicious and quick snack, ideal for an impromptu party, Their unexpected bite is given by the unusual ginger and mustard flavouring.

Attractive Tofu Chicken Patties make both an exciting hors d'oeuvre and a tasty main meal.

Prepare them by first wrapping the tofu in a dry cloth to expel the moisture. Crumble the dried tofu and then combine it with the ground chicken and cornflour in a bowl. Knead thoroughly until all the ingredients are well mixed.

Season with salt and pepper and divide the mixture into 12-16 patties. Dredge one side of each with flour. Spread a shiso leaf on the floured side of each patty. Heat the oil in a frying pan and fry the patties (shiso side first) until golden. Turn over and fry on the other side. Repeat for each batch of patties making sure that the cooked patties stay warm.

Serve the patties hot with shoyu (soy sauce) and mustard. A crisp salad or seasonal vegetables go well with this dish. Crusty garlic bread is also an excellent accompaniment.

As an alternative, or if shiso leaves or nori are too difficult to obtain, drop the tofu mixture by spoonfuls into the frying pan and sprinkle minced parsley or celery over the top of the patties. When the first side is done, turn the patties over and fry the other side until golden brown.

As a further variation, other meat such as minced beef, lamb or pork can be substituted for the chicken.

STUFFED MARROW

1 small marrow – 1½-2lb (700-900g)
3½oz (100g) okara
1 egg
¼ teaspoon salt
1 tablespoon shoyu (soy sauce)

8 tablespoons minced mixed vegetables (carrots, string beans, celery, mushrooms etc.)
1 tablespoon sugar
2 tablespoons salad oil

As a light supper or interesting hors d'oeuvres, marrow stuffed with an okara mixture is both unusual and delicious.

To prepare, peel the marrow, remove the seeds and cut into eight rings. Crumble the okara with your fingers until it is free of lumps. If it is too wet, stir-fry it in a clean, ungreased frying pan first. Cool and mix it with all the other ingredients in a bowl and mix well. Pack the filling tightly into the centre of each ring. Bring a steamer to a rolling boil. Place the marrow rings in a bowl inside the steamer and steam for 30 minutes or until the marrow is cooked.

Serve immediately with a crisp salad and new potatoes, if in season.

This recipe will serve four people as a main dish or eight people as an hors d'oeuvre.

TOFU GRATIN WITH EGGPLANT

1lb 5oz (600g) tofu
3 large ripe tomatoes
8 small or 3 large aubergines
2 tablespoons olive oil

1½oz (42g) grated Parmesan cheese
1 teaspoon salt

To prepare this tasty, nutritious savoury dish, first wrap the tofu in a cloth and set aside for 20 minutes to allow it to become firm.

When it is ready, cut the tofu into slices about ⅓in (8mm) thick and spread them on a new cloth to expel the moisture. Chop the aubergines and tomatoes into slices the same thickness as the tofu.

Heat enough oil to deep fry the aubergines and cook briefly, then remove and drain on paper towels. Arrange the tofu, deep-fried aubergines and tomatoes in layers in a baking dish and sprinkle over the olive oil and finally, the Parmesan cheese. Bake at 375°F (190°C) for 30 minutes or until the top is browned.

This delicious dish can be served alone or with hot crusty bread or rice. This quantity makes a substantial snack for six people or a main meal for four.

LASAGNE

For sauce:
1 pint (0.5l) tomato sauce
½ pint (0.25l) water
1 clove garlic, crushed
½ teaspoon oregano
1 teaspoon basil
⅛ teaspoon thyme
1 teaspoon salt
2 teaspoons sugar
1 tablespoon salad oil

For filling:
2 eggs
1lb (453g) tofu
½ teaspoon salt
6 tbsp grated Parmesan cheese
¼ cup finely chopped parsley

Lasagne
12oz (340g) lasagne noodles,
    cooked and drained
8oz (226g) Mozzarella cheese,
    grated

This is a tasty Italian-style meal, where noodles are mixed with protein-rich tofu and topped with a spicy sauce.

To prepare, mix all the sauce ingredients together in

La dolce vita Tofu in Lasagne makes a healthy and hearty Italian-style meal.

a saucepan and simmer the mixture for about one hour.

While this is cooking mix together all the ingredients for the filling and set aside. When the sauce is ready, take a greased baking dish 7½in x 11½in and spread a layer (roughly one third) of the lasagne noodles over the base.

Pour a third of the sauce over the noodles and then spread half the tofu mixture over this. Repeat with a second layer of noodles, sauce and the remaining tofu-cheese mixture. Spread over the last layer of noodles and sauce, cover the baking dish with foil and bake at 325°F (160°C) for about 30 minutes.

Remove the foil and sprinkle the shredded Mozzarella cheese over the lasagne. Bake for a further 15 minutes or until the cheese is bubbling.

As a tasty luncheon or supper dish, serve the lasagne, cut into squares, with a fresh salad and glass of cold white Italian wine.

TOFU CHICKEN DUMPLINGS

8¾oz (250g) minced chicken
1 tablespoon cornflour
2 tablespoons minced onion
10oz (283g) tofu, pressed and
    crumbled

½ teaspoon salt
¼ teaspoon pepper
Chicken broth
Parsley to garnish

For a light luncheon special, this tofu dish is simple and quick to prepare. Combine all the ingredients except the stock and the parsley and set the mixture aside.

Bring eight cups of water to the boil in a large saucepan adding one tablespoon salt. Using a wooden spatula, scoop out a little of the dough and scrape it off with the plastic spatula to form a small dumpling about 1in (2.5cm) in length and immediately drop it into the water. Quickly repeat the process, rinsing the rubber spatula with cold water as soon as it begins to stick.

As the dumplings cook, they will rise to the surface. When the surface is covered with dumplings, let them cook for a further five minutes and then remove them from the water with a slotted spoon and set aside in a warm, covered bowl. Repeat the process with the rest of the dough. Lastly, warm the chicken broth correcting the seasoning to taste. Place five to seven dumplings in individual soup bowls, pour the broth over them, decorate with parsley and serve.

TOFU POTATO DUMPLINGS

Dumplings with a difference
Tofu and potato make this simple dish delicious and nutritious.

10oz (283g) tofu, pressed and
    crumbled
3 medium-sized potatoes,
    grated and well-drained

1 egg
2 tablespoons flour
8 tablespoons minced parsley
Salt and pepper to taste

These protein-rich potato dumplings are both nutritious and quick and simple to prepare. First, combine the tofu, grated potatoes, flour, egg and parsley in a blender and mix until smooth. Season the dough with salt and pepper to taste. Using two wet spoons, scoop up the dough to form dumplings about the thickness of a finger 1½in (4cm) long and drop them into boiling water. The dumplings usually require about 15 minutes' cooking time but test and taste to make sure the potatoes are soft and the texture is smooth. Cook a little longer if necessary.

Served in clear soup, the tofu dumplings make a delicious light meal in themselves. Alternatively, add cooked vegetables and ham to make a hearty meal or serve them with gravy as an interesting accompaniment to any meat dish.

PORK PIE WITH TOFU MOUSSE

For pie crust:
8¾oz (250g) flour
¼lb (113g) butter
1 small egg
A pinch of salt
2 tablespoons cold water

For mousse:
8¾oz (250g) tofu
7oz (198g) mushrooms, wiped
  clean, stemmed and minced
2 tablespoons cornflour
4 tablespoons minced shallots
  or onion
½ teaspoon salt
⅛ teaspooon black pepper
4 tablespoons brandy
1½oz (42g) breadcrumbs
1 egg white
½ teaspoon thyme
3 tablespoons minced parsley
1lb (453g) pork steak
Salt and pepper
4 tablespoons salad oil
1 egg yolk

To create this delicious and rewarding dish, first make the pie crust, following the recipe given for short crust pastry on p.103. Chill the pastry for at least two hours.

For the filling, crumble the tofu into a saucepan with ½ teaspoon salt. Bring to the boil and cook over a high heat for three minutes. The tofu must then be poured through a cloth and pressed firmly to expel as much moisture as possible. Set it aside.

Next, sauté the shallot in oil until translucent, add the mushrooms and sauté for another three minutes. Sprinkle brandy over them and bring back to the boil. Add the cornflour, dissolved in a little cold water, cook for one minute and set aside.

Take the pork steak, season it with salt and black pepper and fry in a little oil over a high heat until brown on all sides. Set this aside.

To prepare the mousse, crumble the tofu into a bowl and mix it with the mushrooms, breadcrumbs, egg white, thyme and parsley until all are well combined. Divide the pastry dough into two parts, one piece double the size of the other. Roll out both pieces of dough into an oval shape ⅛in (3mm) thick.

Spread half of the tofu mousse over the smaller piece, leaving ⅔in (1.6cm) pastry margin all around. Place the

Perfect party and picnic fare
Pork Pie with Tofu Mousse will satisfy the most fastidious epicure's tastes.

fillet in the centre and cover it with the rest of the tofu mixture, making sure the surface is smooth. Cover with the other piece of pastry, pressing firmly around the sides to close the loaf. Cut off the excess dough. Brush the pastry with egg yolk and decorate with pastry ribbons cut from the excess dough. Brush again with egg yolk and leave the loaf to stand for 20 minutes to allow the filling to set.

For the last stage, preheat the oven to 375°F (190°C) and bake the pie for 25-30 minutes until golden brown.

BROILED TOFU WITH MISO SAUCE

1lb (453g) tofu
Sesame oil for frying

Miso sauce:
8 tablespoons miso (soybean paste)

1¾oz (50g) sugar
4 tablespoons sake or sherry
2 tablespoons grated ginger root
1 tablespoon ground sesame seeds

Protein-rich tofu in a delicate miso-sesame sauce gives this dish a distinctive Japanese flavour. And therefore, if possible do try and obtain authentic miso, sake and sesame oil and seeds as any substitute impairs the taste of this dish. All of them should be available from specialty Oriental or health food stores. As miso or soybean paste tends to be salty, vary the quantity suggested here, according to taste.

Prepare the tofu first, cutting it into pieces about ½in (1.3cm) thick. Wrap the tofu squares in a dry cloth to expel the moisture. Heat the sesame oil in a frying pan and fry the tofu on both sides until brown.

In a saucepan, combine all the sauce ingredients and cook over a low heat for about 30 minutes, stirring constantly to avoid sticking. Add water or sake if the sauce is too thick. Cover the base of a casserole with the fried tofu. Spread the miso sauce over it, sprinkle with sesame seeds and bake in a hot oven until the sauce begins to bubble. Serve at once, with a colourful salad and whole-meal bread as an accompaniment.

A Japanese delicacy The ethnic ingredients – tofu, sesame, miso and sake - flavour this delicious oriental dish.

VEGETARIAN QUICHE

3 medium onions, sliced
2 tablespoons salad oil
4 eggs
1 lb (453g) tofu
1 ½ teaspoons salt

¼ teaspoon pepper
9oz (255g) shredded cheese
19in (48cm) piecrust (p.103)
Broccoli, steamed, for garnish

To prepare this delicious protein-rich vegetarian meal in just a few simple steps, heat the oil, gently sauté the onion slices until transparent and set aside.

Mix the eggs, tofu, salt and pepper together in a blender until smooth and then, by hand, stir in the shredded cheese. Spread the sautéed onions over the bottom of the pie shell and pour the tofu mixture over them. Decorate the surface with tiny steamed broccoli florets.

Preheat the oven to 350°F (180°C) for 45 minutes or until a knife inserted in the quiche comes out clean.

Tofu quiche lends itself to endless modifications by substituting any combination of steamed vegetables for the onions. The quiche should be cut into wedges and can be served either hot or cold. A salad or fresh vegetable is a suitable accompaniment to this dish.

TOFU KNISHES

Knish-crust:
8 tablespoons mashed potatoes
2 tablespoons salad oil
¼ teaspoon salt
6oz (170g) plain flour
½ teaspoon baking powder
½ pint (⅛l) water

¼ onion, chopped into chunks
1 tablespoon salad oil
8¾oz (250g) mashed tofu
1 tablespoon shoyu (soy sauce)
½ teaspoon ginger
½ teaspoon minced garlic
¼ teaspoon curry powder

Filling:
¼lb (113g) cabbage, chopped

Spicy and substantial
Golden brown Tofu Knishes make a tasty supper or lunch-time meal.

For this delicious and substantial tofu dish, first prepare the knish-crust. In a large bowl, mix the potatoes, oil and salt until combined. Sift in the flour and baking powder and then add the water, stirring until all ingredients are evenly distributed and the mixture has become a thick dough. Continue kneading until the dough is quite smooth and then set it aside for 30 minutes while preparing the filling.

Pour the salad oil into a pan and gently sauté the chopped cabbage and onion. These must be cooked until tender but not brown. Add the tofu, soy sauce, ginger, garlic and curry, mix well and then set aside to cool.

The dough should now be ready to shape. Pinch off small pieces of dough, ¾in (1.8cm) in diameter and roll into 4in (10cm) circles about ⅛in (3mm) thick.
For accuracy, you may wish to cut out a paper circle to the precise measurements and use this for a guide. Place a spoonful of filling in the centre of the dough circle, fold over the sides and pinch the edges together.

Preheat the oven to 375°F (190°C) and arrange the knishes on a greased baking pan, seam side up, and bake for about 25 minutes, or until the knishes are light brown.

Tofu knishes can be served hot or cold with salad or fresh vegetables.

A savoury protein-rich queen of quiches Served hot or cold, it is sure to please.

Seafoood special Baked Fish with Tofu White Sauce (see recipe overleaf) is a casserole in a class of its own.

BAKED FISH WITH TOFU WHITE SAUCE

16 tablespoons water
16 tablespoons dry white wine
Juice of ½ lemon
2 bay leaves
1 small onion, sliced
1¼ tablespoons brandy
5 peppercorns
1 teaspoon salt
2lb 4oz (1kg) white fish fillets
12oz (340g) fresh spinach leaves

For the white sauce:
10oz (283g) tofu
3 tablespoons butter
3 tablespoons flour
1 pint (½l) fish stock
½ pint (¼l) milk
Juice of ½ lemon
Salt and pepper to taste
3 tablespoons chopped dill

To create this exotic fish dish with its exquisitely tangy tofu sauce requires careful preparation but is effort well-repaid. Mix the tofu in a blender until smooth and set aside.

Pour the water, wine, lemon juice and brandy into a large pan and add the bayleaves, onions, peppercorns and salt. Bring to the boil. Place the fish fillets in the boiling liquid and cook over a low heat for 15 minutes. Remove the fish fillets, strain the stock and set both aside separately in a warm place. Parboil the well-cleaned spinach in salted water, drain and cut into bite-sized pieces and set aside.

The next step is preparing the sauce. For this, melt the butter in a frying pan, sift in the flour and cook for 2 minutes, stirring constantly with a wooden spoon to avoid lumps and make sure that the mixture is smooth and does not burn. Add the fish stock, milk, salt and pepper and cook over a low heat, still stirring, until it is thick and smooth. Remove from the heat and add the tofu purée and lemon to the white sauce, mix thoroughly. Preheat the oven to 400°F (200°C), butter a gratin dish, cover the base with the cooked fish, spread the spinach over the fish and pour over the sauce. Sprinkle with dill and bake in the oven until the sauce begins to bubble and the top is browned.

As a speedier alternative, make sure the cooked fish is well warm, pour the sauce over and quickly brown under the grill.

FRIED TOFU WITH GREEN ONION

1lb (453g) tofu
2 eggs
8 tablespoons shredded red chilli pepper
8 tablespoons green spring onion, cut into thin strips
1 tablespoon flour

For the sauce:
½ pint (¼l) soup stock
4 tablespoons shoyu (soy sauce)
4 tablespoons sugar
1 teaspoon crushed garlic
2 teaspoons grated ginger root
½ teaspoon chilli powder
½ pear or apple, grated

Golden cakes of nutritious tofu, spiced with chili and onion and served with a piquant sauce make this a dish to delight the eye and palate. As a snack or the basis of a main meal, it is sure to please.

The tofu is prepared first. Cut the 1lb block into eight oblong slices and wrap them in a dry cloth. When the moisture is expelled, unwrap and sprinkle the slices with a little salt. Decorate each slice with a few strips of spring onion and set aside.

Beat the eggs and flour together until smooth and dip each tofu slice in the mixture. Grease a frying pan or ideally, a griddle. Gently fry the slices on each side until the coating is firm. It is important that they are cooked over a low heat as this will ensure they retain the bright yellow egg colour which makes them so attractive.

For the sauce, mix the soup stock, shoyu and sugar in a saucepan and bring to the boil. Take off the heat and add the other ingredients and spices. Divide the sauce between four individual bowls. Place a tofu slice in each and the dish is ready to serve.

A crisp and colourful side salad and hot crusty bread are excellent accompaniments to this dish.

If any of your guests have an aversion to onions or a subtle change of flavour is desired, vary the spring onion decoration by substituting young celery leaves, watercress or minced parsley.

A simple, healthy dish Fried Tofu with Green Onion is as tasty as it is pleasing to the eye.

TOFU WITH MEAT SAUCE

20oz (600g) tofu
2 tablespoons minced onion
1 tablespoon minced garlic
3 tablespoons vegetable oil
7oz (198g) lean minced pork or
 beef
1 teaspoon salt

½ teaspoon pepper
8 tablespoons soup stock or
 water
3 tablespoons sour cream
2 tablespoons cornflour,
 dissolved in 2 tablespoons
 water

In this delicious protein-rich dish, the flavour of tofu is enhanced by a sauce that is both versatile and easy to prepare.

First, heat the oil in a frying pan and cook the garlic and onion for a few minutes over a medium heat. Add the ground meat, brown and season with salt and pepper. Add the water and sour cream and bring the mixture back to the boil. Stir in the dissolved cornflour and cook until thickened.

Next, in a saucepan, boil ½ pint (0.28l) of water mixed with two teaspoons of salt and cook the tofu in it for three minutes. Drain and keep warm. Cut the tofu into four portions. Pour the sauce over it and serve piping hot.

Using this basic method, a variety of flavours can be achieved by substituting miso (fermented bean-paste) or soy sauce for the salt, adding cayenne pepper, tomato paste or anchovy paste.

This tofu dish can be served as a starter or, complemented by seasonal vegetables, as a main meal.

FINE CHICKEN FRICASSE WITH TOFU

1 whole chicken
10oz (283g) tofu, pressed
1 medium-sized carrot
1 stalk of celery
3-4 sprigs parsley
1 medium-sized onion
8½oz (240g) chopped and
 drained canned asparagus
½ pint (¼l) milk
8 tablespoons white wine

1 quart (1l) water
1oz (28g) breadcrumbs
1 egg
Salt and pepper to taste
3 bay leaves

Cream sauce:
2 tablespoons butter
3 tablespoons flour
2 egg yolks, beaten

A rich and colourful chicken dish that delights both the palate and eye, this tofu specialty would grace any elegant dinner table.

For its preparation, place the chicken in a large pan together with the wine, carrot, onion, celery, parsley, bay leaves, salt and pepper. Cook this over a medium heat

A colourful chicken dish
with a difference Chicken,
tofu, asparagus and white
wine make this protein-rich
gourmet fare.

until the chicken is tender, occasionally skimming the broth. Lift the chicken from the broth and remove both skin and bones. Cut the chicken meat into small pieces and mix with the tofu in a blender until smooth. Pour the mixture into another bowl and add the breadcrumbs and egg, mixing thoroughly. Season to taste with salt and pepper. Next, take the carrot, onion and celery stalk out of the broth, chop coarsely and set aside. Strain the broth and reserving ¾ pint (0.42l) for the cream sauce, bring the remaining liquid to the boil. Drop spoonfulls of the chicken tofu mixture into the boiling broth and allow to simmer for 15 minutes.

While this is cooking, prepare the cream sauce by melting the butter in a saucepan and gradually adding the flour and reserved broth. Let the mixture simmer for five minutes, stirring constantly. A little extra liquid may be added if the sauce becomes too thick. Remove the pan from the heat and add the egg yolks, stirring until thoroughly mixed. Season and add the cooked dumplings, vegetables and asparagus. Gently reheat the fricassee taking care that the sauce does not boil.

The dish can be attractively served on a circular bed of rice, sprinkled with chopped parsley.

TOFU MARROW DUMPLINGS

10oz (283g) tofu
Marrow from 2lb (0.9kg) of beef
    bone (about 8oz (226g)
    loosely measured)
1 egg
2 tablespoons flour
1 teaspoon salt

2 tablespoons finely chopped
    parsley
4 pints (2.2l) water
2 bay leaves
5 pepper corns
Okra for garnish

1. This unusual combination of beef marrow and tofu makes a delicious main dish. To prepare, place the tofu under a heavy weight for 20 minutes before crumbling. Meanwhile extract the marrow from the bone and clean well in a colander.

2. Mash the marrow finely with a fork and mix it in a bowl with the tofu, parsley, and salt.

3. Add the egg and gradually stir in the flour until the dough is firm enough to form into balls. Boil the water in a saucepan and add the bay leaves and peppercorns.

4. Shape the dough and drop the balls into the boiling water, reducing the heat immediately, and simmer for 20 minutes. Test and cook for a little longer if necessary. Cooked vegetables, if required, can be added at this stage. Finally, strain the broth and correct the seasoning with salt and pepper. Place five to seven marrow balls into individual soup bowls. Pour the clear broth over them, garnish with okra and the dish is ready to serve.

STEAMED TOFU SANDWICH

20oz (600g) tofu
8oz (226g) minced pork/chicken
2 tablespoons minced onion
2 tablespoons fresh green
  peppercorns, crushed
1 tablespoon cornflour
½ teaspoon salt for filling
½ teaspoon salt for tofu

For mustard sauce
8 tablespoons mayonnaise
2 tablespoons hot mustard
1 tablespoon Worcester sauce
2 tablespoons sherry
1 teaspoon curry powder
3 tablespoons milk

For this unusual sandwich that is bursting with protein, first cut the tofu into eight slices or rounds about ½in (13mm) thick. Place them on a cloth, cover with another cloth and leave to stand for 15 minutes, changing cloths

A zesty sandwich Here mild tofu is combined with a spicy filling and coated in a mustard sauce.

if necessary to absorb the maximum amount of moisture. (If cutting rounds, reserve any remaining tofu for the filling). Sprinkle salt evenly over the slices and set aside. In a bowl, mix together the minced meat, onion, green peppercorns, cornflour and any remaining tofu and mix well. Season with ½ teaspoon salt and divide the mixture into four portions. Dredge cornflour over the tofu slices and sandwich the filling between the slices keeping the dredged side inside. Bring the steamer to a full boil, reduce the heat and steam the tofu sandwiches for 12 minutes or until the meat filling is done. While the sandwiches are cooking, prepare the sauce, by blending all the ingredients together in a bowl. Serve the sandwiches piping hot with the mustard sauce and an accompanying salad for a highly nutritious meal.

TOFU CRABMEAT GRATIN

10oz (283g) tofu
3 tablespoons butter
3oz (85g) sliced onion
3oz (85g) sliced celery
3oz (85g) carrot, cut into strips
½ teaspoon salt
⅛ teaspoon pepper
3 tablespoons butter
2 tablespoons flour
1¼ tablespoons brandy

½ pint (¼l) fish stock
½ pint (¼l) milk
7oz (198g) shredded cooked
   crabmeat
1 stick crabmeat
3 tablespoons finely chopped
   parsley
1 tablespoon finely chopped
   fresh tarragon

To prepare this delicate and luxurious seafood dish, first wrap the tofu in a cloth and leave to stand for 15 minutes.

Fry the onion, celery and carrot with butter in a pan until translucent and season with salt and pepper. When cooked, place on some kitchen roll to drain.

In a separate frying pan, melt another three tablespoons butter, add the flour and cook for two minutes, stirring constantly to avoid burning.

Add the brandy and continue cooking over a low heat. Pour in the fish stock and milk and cook for five minutes until smooth, stirring constantly.

Dice the tofu and add this, together with the fried vegetables, crabmeat, parsley and tarragon to the pan. Simmer for two minutes and then season to taste. Pour the mixture into four individual shallow dishes or, as an attractive alternative, cleaned scallop shells.

Just before serving, top each with a quarter of the crabmeat stick and grill until browned. Thin slices of lightly buttered brown bread go well with this dish.

VEGETABLE SOUFFLE

10oz (283g) mashed tofu
8 tablespoons wheat germ
5oz (142g) cooked, drained
   green peas
½ pint (¼l) milk
1 tablespoon cornflour
3 egg yolks

3 egg whites
1 onion, chopped
7oz (198g) sliced mushrooms
1 tablespoon salad oil
3 tablespoons chopped parsley
1 tablespoon white wine (optional)
½ teaspoon salt

To prepare this delicious, light, vegetable soufflé first sauté the onions and mushrooms in oil until transparent. Remove the pan from the heat and add the parsley, wine, salt, mashed tofu, wheat germ and peas. Set aside.

Next, mix the milk and cornflour together in a saucepan and cook over a low heat, stirring constantly until the mixture has thickened. Lightly beat three egg yolks in a bowl and stir in a little of the hot sauce. Pour in the

Decorative dishes Tofu
Crabmeat Gratin attractively
served in scallop shells and
Vegetable Soufflé can make
ideal meals for one.

remainder, mix well and return to the saucepan. Cook
over a low heat, again stirring constantly, until thickened.
Take care not to boil the mixture. Stir the sauce into the
tofu and vegetables and set aside to cool.

Whip the egg whites until stiff and fold in the tofu
mixture. Grease and dust a straight-sided baking dish or
individual cups with wheat-germ and gently spoon in the
soufflé. Bake at 350°F (180°C) for about 45 minutes or until
the soufflé is set and lightly browned.

To serve, prepare a crisp salad or fresh vegetables as an
accompaniment if required.

TOFU BURGERS

7oz (198g) mashed tofu
16 tablespoons cooked rice
8 tablespoons chopped onion
3½oz (99g) plain flour
½ teaspoon basil

¼ teaspoon oregano
1 teaspoon salt
⅛ teaspoon pepper
1 egg

These protein-rich burgers are perfect fare for the vegetarian and quick and simple to prepare.

First, mix all the ingredients together in a large bowl and shape into six portions. Heat a little salad oil in a pan and fry each until the centre is cooked and the surface is browned.

This quick, tasty dish is then ready to serve with ketchup, mustard and pickles, accompanied by bread, salad or vegetables if required.

ITALIAN TOFU

Tofu balls:
10oz (283g) tofu
1½oz (42g) chopped walnuts
½ small onion, chopped
¾oz (21g) dry breadcrumbs
1 egg
2 tablespoons chopped parsley

½ teaspoon salt
Oil for deep frying

Sauce:
12 tablespoons tomato sauce
¼ teaspoon oregano

Italian Tofu with its subtle continental flavour requires just a few quick steps to prepare. For the tofu balls, mix together all the ingredients by hand until well combined. Set aside.

Heat the oil for deep-frying. Shape the tofu mixture into 1½in balls and fry until they are light brown in colour and the centres are firm and dry. Remove the balls from the pan and drain on paper towels. Keep the balls warm.

For the sauce, heat the tomato sauce and oregano together in a saucepan. Pour the sauce over the balls and serve with pasta, salad and a glass of Italian wine.

Continental fare
Complement this tofu dish with a salad and wine and pasta if desired.

DEEP-FRIED TOFU SANDWICH

20oz (600g) tofu
4 small slices of ham
4 small slices of cheese
8 tablespoons minced pork/beef
1 teaspoon grated ginger root

1 tablespoon mayonnaise
4 thin slices of onion
8 tablespoons cornflour
Vegetable oil for deep frying
8 tablespoons flaked tuna

¼ teaspoon salt

Salt and lemon juice as a condiment

This is a quick and tasty meal which includes both a meat and fish filling.

To prepare the sandwich, cut the block of tofu into 12 slices. Drain the slices on kitchen roll to expel the maximum amount of moisture. Slit each tofu slice to form a pocket and set aside.

Mix the ground meat, ginger and salt in one bowl, the tuna and mayonnaise in another. Fill four tofu slices with ham and cheese and the remaining four with the minced meat or tuna and onion filling. Coat each sandwich thoroughly with cornflour, heat the oil and deep-fry quickly over a high heat.

Serve piping hot with a seasoning of salt and lemon juice.

CHICKEN WITH CURRY STUFFING

Chicken with Curry Stuffing
The spicy tofu filling makes all the difference to this tasty dish, which is based on Chicken Kiev.

10oz (283g) tofu, well pressed
4 breast fillets of chicken, about 7oz (198g) each
2¾oz (77g) minced parsley
2¾oz (77g) minced celery
2oz (57g) minced onion
1 egg
1 teaspoon salt

A pinch of pepper
1 tablespoon curry powder
1 egg
3½oz (99g) plain flour
3oz (85g) breadcrumbs
Salad oil for deep-frying

The spicy tofu curry stuffing combined with the milder flavour of tender white chicken makes this a delicious and unusual gourmet dish which also requires remarkably little preparation. Fresh herbs and freshly-ground curry powder taste best if they can be obtained. Begin by slitting the chicken fillets with a sharp knife to form pouches. Set these aside.

To prepare the filling, crumble the tofu in a bowl and add the parsley, celery, onion, a third of the breacrumbs and egg. Season the filling to taste with salt, pepper and curry powder, ensuring all ingredients are well mixed.

Fill the chicken pouches with the stuffing to within ½in (12mm) of their edge. Gently press the pouches to close the edges and evenly distribute the filling. Roll each pouch in flour, dip in beaten egg and then roll in the breadcrumbs until well-coated.

Finally, in a deep frying pan, heat enough salad oil to cover the chicken pouches.Deep fry the pouches for 10 minutes over a medium heat until crisp and golden. Lift the pouches gently from the pan and drain well on kitchen roll.

The spicy chicken fillets are then ready to serve. A fresh salad and new potatoes are a suitable accompaniment if required.

TOFU FLAMBE

10oz (283g) tofu
2½oz (70g) flour
3 tablespoons minced onion
½ pint (¼l) cream
8 tablespoons brandy

1 teaspoon salt
A pinch of pepper
1 tablespoon lemon juice
2 tablespoons butter

To prepare Tofu Flambé, press the tofu under a heavy weight for 20 minutes to expel the moisture and cut into four slices. Sprinkle with lemon, dust with flour and sauté

on each side until brown. Set the tofu aside in a warm place.

For the sauce, melt the butter in a pan and fry the onion for one minute. Add the cream and bring to the boil. Season with pepper and salt to taste. Lay the tofu in the warm sauce. Pour the brandy into a large metal ladle, warm gently over a flame and ignite. Pour the flaming brandy over the tofu. Stir the sauce gently to burn off all the alcohol.

As the flame dies, prepare hot plates and serve the exotic tofu dish.

A delectable dish Flaming brandy adds a romantic touch to this tofu meal.

TUNA SALAD IN TOMATO ASPIC RING

1lb (450g) tofu	I pint (0.56l) water
2 courgettes	2 chicken stock cubes
1 small eggplant	Salt and pepper to taste
2 stalks celery	3 bay leaves
A handful of string beans	**For marinade:**
2 medium-sized onions	8 tablespoons salad oil
2 large green peppers	8 tablespoons cider vinegar
For broth:	1 tablespoon sugar

Bright and nutritious Tuna Salad and Tomato Aspic Ring make attractive, contrasting table centrepieces.

To prepare, this healthy and unusual salad of cooked vegetables, first sprinkle the tofu with a teaspoon of salt and steam over a high heat for ten minutes. Set aside to cool. Clean and chop the vegetables. Mix the broth ingredients in a large pan and bring to the boil. Cook the vegetables in the broth for ten minutes. Remove the pan from the heat and mix in the marinade ingredients. Cut the tofu into cubes and add these to the pan. Chill. Finally spoon out the tofu and vegetables and arrange them on a dish. Garnish with parsley and serve.

COOKED SALAD WITH TOFU

For the salad:	1 tablespoon hot mustard
10oz (283g) tofu	2 tablespooons mayonnaise
6oz (170g) canned tuna, drained	Salt and pepper
Juice of one lemon	Chopped parsley to garnish
1 tablespoon minced capers	**For the aspic:**
2 tablespoons minced pickled	4½ tablespoons (40g)
cucumbers	powdered gelatine
2 tablespoons minced onion	½ pint (¼l) fish broth

½ pint (¼l) tomato juice
8 tablespoons dry white wine

1 tablespoon cider vinegar
1 tablespoon paprika

To prepare this spectacular party piece, first wrap the tofu in a large cloth and press for ten minutes. Then, dice half of it into ⅕in (5mm) cubes. Set aside. Soak the gelatine in the ¼ cup broth and mix the rest of the broth with the tomato juice and wine in a saucepan. Bring to the boil and immediately remove from the heat. Add the soaked gelatine and stir until it dissolves. Pour in the vinegar and add the paprika, salt and pepper to season the jelly. Set aside to cool.

Meanwhile, rinse out a ring mould in cold water. Pour in just enough of the cooled gelatine solution to cover the base of the mould. Sprinkle with a handful of the tofu cubes and set in the refrigerator to chill. Cool the remaining gelatine until the mixture begins to thicken and gently mix in the rest of the tofu cubes. Pour this into the ring mould and again refrigerate.

For the filling, mash the other half of the tofu with a fork and flake in the tuna. Add the lemon juice, capers, pickles, onion, mustard and mayonnaise. Mix thoroughly and season with salt and pepper.

When the aspic is set, turn it out onto a serving dish and spoon in the filling. Garnish with parsley.

TOFU WAKAME

3 tablespoons vinegar
3 tablespoons sesame oil
2 tablespoons salad oil
1 teaspoon sugar
2 tablespoons ground sesame seeds
½ teaspoon mustard
10oz (283g) tofu

2oz (56g) cucumber
7oz (198g) wakamé (seaweed, available dried from Japanese speciality stores

For dressing:
3 tablespooons shoyu (soy sauce)

Calorie-free wakamé which is a tasty and highly nutritious component of many Japanese dishes, is here complemented by a light vinegary dressing.

Soften the wakamé first, by soaking it in tepid water for around 20 minutes. Chop, taking care to remove any tough sections, and set aside.

Wrap the tofu in a cloth and allow to stand for 15 minutes. Then cut into bite-sized pieces. Thinly slice the cucumber, sprinkle with a little salt and leave until beads of moisture appear. Press to expel the liquid.

On a dish, arrange the tofu, cucumber and wakamé. Just before serving, beat all the ingredients for the dressing in a bowl. Pour the dressing over the salad and serve with French bread warmed in the oven.

The light and nutritious salad is perfect summer fare.

Seasonal salads Tofu can
make a whole variety of salads
.even more nutritious.
Clockwise: Cooked Salad with
Tofu, Deviled Tofu Salad, Tofu
Tuna Salad in Tomato Aspic
Ring, Tofu Seafood Salad and
Tofu Wakamé Salad.

CHILLED TOFU WITH GREEN SAUCE

1lb (453g) tofu
8 tablespoons dry white wine
2 teaspoons salt

For the sauce:
16 tablespoons finely chopped
   fresh herbs (parsley, mint,
   oregano, dill, chives etc.)
1 tablespoon minced pickles

1 tablespoon minced green olives
2 tablespoons salad oil
2 tablespoons cider vinegar
½ teaspoon salt
¼ teaspoon pepper

To garnish:
Several slices of stuffed olives

Marinated tofu in a tangy sauce is a perfect summer dish that is both refreshing, healthy and very simple to create. Prepare the tofu first. In a saucepan, bring one cup (¼l) water to the boil and add the salt. Place the tofu carefully in the pan and cook covered for two minutes. Drain and slide the tofu slice into a bowl. Pour over the wine, cover the bowl with clingfilm and place in the refrigerator.

When the tofu is well chilled, pat it dry with a kitchen towel. Set it on a serving dish and cut into slices about ⅓in (8mm) thick.

For the sauce, combine all the remaining ingredients in a bowl and mix thoroughly. Pour this over the tofu and garnish with olive slices.

Serve as the centrepiece of a salad meal accompanied by colourful fresh vegetables and bread or new potatoes. Alone, it can also serve as an attractive hors d'oeuvre or snack.

While appetites may vary, this recipe is designed to serve three or four people.

DEVILLED TOFU SALAD

2 tablespoons tofu mayonnaise
   (p.46)
2 teaspoons cider vinegar
¼ teaspoon dry mustard
¼ teaspoon salt

¼ teaspoon garlic powder
¼ teaspoon turmeric
14oz (397g) tofu, drained and
   pressed

This deliciously spicy salad could well prove a novelty here, but in America it has long been a popular classic of the soy delicatessen.

To prepare, mix all the ingredients, except the tofu, in a bowl. Add the tofu and mix it in with a spatula until it breaks down into small pieces. Chill.

Serve the salad as a main dish on a bed of lettuce accompanied by jacket potatoes or a granary loaf.

Alternatively, spread it on crusty rolls or wholemeal bread as a tasty and nutritious sandwich filling, perfect for the school lunch box.

TOFU SEAFOOD SALAD

10oz (283g) tofu
3 tablespoons soyu (soy sauce)
10oz (283g) whole shrimps, fresh or frozen
10oz (283g) scallops, fresh or frozen
5oz (142g) octopus, cooked
3½oz (99g) fresh string beans
4 stalks watercress

For dressing:
4 tablespoons finely chopped dill
¼ pint (142ml) cider vinegar
¼ pint (142ml) salad oil
½ teaspoon salt
½ teaspoon sugar
⅛ teaspoon white pepper

Seafood lovers are sure to be delighted by this protein-rich salad dish which combines a marinated mixture of shrimp, octopus and scallops with string beans and tofu.

Prepare the tofu well in advance, simmering it in salted water for five minutes. Drain on a plate and pour over the shoyu. Wrap in clingfilm, ensuring it is airtight and chill in the refrigerator for at least two hours.

Meanwhile, clean the shrimp, discard the shells and remove the veins. Cook in salted water for two minutes until the colour changes to bright pink. Parboil the scallops by adding them to the boiling shrimp. Drain. Add the octopus, chopped into bite-sized pieces and chill in the refrigerator. Next, clean the string beans and cut into 1in (2.5cm) pieces. Parboil in salted water, then cool immediately under cold running water. This will ensure the beans retain their colour. Drain and set aside.

In a bowl, combine all the ingredients for the dressing. Marinate the seafood and string beans in the dressing and set aside to absorb the marinade flavour until required.

Just before serving, spoon out the beans and seafood and arrange in a large salad bowl. Cut the tofu into bite-sized pieces and sprinkle these over the seafood. Pour over the marinade, garnish with watercress and serve. Fresh crusty bread goes well with this salad and a glass of cold white wine adds a festive touch to the meal.

A scrumptious seafood salad
Rich in protein and low in cholesterol, this dish is ideal slimming fare.

Delicate Desserts And Delicious Cakes

Apple Cake * Refrigerator Cheesecake * Tofu Cream Pudding * Chocolate Frozen Dessert * Strawberry Frozen Dessert * Frosty Peach Dessert * Flaming Crêpes * Pancakes * Soft Spice Cookies * Holiday Fruit Cake * Sweet Potato Pie * Vanilla Bavarian Cream * Coconut Tofu Dessert * Tofu Cinnamon Buns * Tofu Mango Dessert * Tofu Lemon Dessert * Tofu White Chocolate Cream * Banana Cream Pie * Easy-To-Do Tofu Cheesecake * Tofu Whip * Soy Whip * Crumb Crust * Short Crust * Gingerbread Cookies

DELICATE DESSERTS AND DELICIOUS CAKES

The perfect dessert should be delicate and colourful, a refreshing finale to a tasty meal. The sweets presented here – luscious cheesecakes, creamy pies and frozen delights – are both nutritious and exotic enough to add a festive touch to any dinner party. Also included are a selection of children's tea-time favourites – Soft Spice Cookies, Gingerbread Cookies and a Holiday Fruitcake that is half as fattening and just as delicious as traditional Christmas cake.

APPLE CAKE

10oz (283g) plain flour
1½ teaspoons bicarbonate of
   soda
1 egg
4 tablespoons salad oil
7oz (198g) mashed tofu

6oz (170g) brown sugar
2 teaspoons cinnamon
½ teaspoon salt
1 teaspoon vanilla essence
5¼oz (149g) chopped apples
4½oz (127g) chopped nuts

Apples, nuts and tofu make this cake both delicious and nutritious fare, rich in protein and vitamin C.

To prepare, mix the flour and bicarbonate together in a bowl and set aside. Combine the egg, oil, tofu, sugar, cinnamon, salt and vanilla. Stir this into the flour and lastly, mix in the fruit and nuts. Cook the cake mix in a greased 9in x 13in (22.5cm x 32.5cm) baking tin at 350°F (180°C) for about 35 minutes or until a skewer or knife inserted comes out clean. Serve the cake sprinkled with powdered sugar.

A trio of tempting tofu sweets Refrigerator Cheesecake, Tofu Cream Pudding and Chocolate Frozen Dessert are easy-to-make delicacies you will be proud to serve.

REFRIGERATOR CHEESECAKE

2 tablespoons gelatine
6 tablespoons water
8 tablespoons sugar
12¼oz (347g) tofu
¾ pint (426ml) yoghurt

3oz (85g) cream cheese
½ teaspoon salt
1 teaspoon vanilla essence
1 crumb crust pie shell (p.102)

Tofu cheesecake, less rich and calorific than the traditional recipes, makes a luscious, light and refreshing dessert to end a special meal.

Prepare well in advance by first melting the gelatine in a cup, adding the water, and heating over a low flame or in a microwave. Set aside. Combine the sugar, tofu, yoghurt, cheese, salt and vanilla in a blender and add the melted gelatine. Pour the mixture into the crumb crust shell and chill for at least four hours, or overnight. Before serving, garnish with the fresh fruit of your choice.

TOFU CREAM PUDDING

2¾oz (77g) non-fat milk
    powder
8¾oz (250g) tofu
1 teaspoon vanilla essence
4 tablespoons water

½ teaspoon salt
2 tablespoons cornflour
8 tablespoons sugar
14fl oz (397ml) water

For a milky pudding that is both protein-rich and easy to digest, mix the tofu, milk, vanilla, water and salt in a blender. Set aside and combine the cornflour, sugar and water in a saucepan. Cook until clear and thick. Remove from the heat and add the tofu mixture. Blend and serve.

CHOCOLATE FROZEN DESSERT

10½oz (300g) tofu
3 tablespoons salad oil
4 tablespoons cocoa
3¼oz (92g) brown sugar

1¾oz (50g) butter or margarine
⅛ teaspoon salt
1 teaspoon vanilla essence

To prepare this tasty chocolate dessert which can be kept frozen for up to one month, mix all the ingredients together in a blender. Spoon into a storage container or metal bowl, cover and freeze for about four hours or until the mixture is mushy.

This dessert can be served straight from the freezer but the flavour is enhanced by allowing it to thaw at room temperature for about half an hour.

STRAWBERRY FROZEN DESSERT

1lb (453g) tofu
3¼oz (92g) sugar
3 tablespoons butter or margarine
8¾oz (248g) strawberry jam

4 tablespoons salad oil
⅛ teaspoon salt
1 teaspoon vanilla essence

This strawberry dessert is a luscious sweet that takes only minutes to make. However, it should be prepared well in advance as several hours' freezing time is required.

To prepare, mix all the ingredients together in a blender until smooth. Spoon the tofu mixture into a storage container or metal bowl. Cover and freeze for about four hours. The mixture should be soft and mushy.

Remove and spoon the mixture into dishes, topping each with a whole strawberry. This should serve eight people.

FROSTY PEACH DESSERT

1 egg yolk
6 tablespoons sugar
3 tablespoons salad oil
1¾oz (50g) butter
1 teaspoon vanilla essence

⅛ teaspoon salt
13¼oz (375g) canned peaches, drained
10½oz (300g) mashed tofu

To make this tasty dessert, mix together the egg yolk, oil, butter, vanilla, salt and a third of the drained peaches in a blender until smooth. Pour the mixture into a storage container or metal bowl. Stir in the remaining peaches and freeze until mushy (about four hours).

FLAMING CREPES

Batter for crêpes:
1 egg
8oz (226g) tofu
2.6 fl oz (75ml) milk
1 tablespoon salad oil
1 tablespoon sugar
½ teaspoon vanilla essence
½ teaspoon baking powder
¼ teaspoon salt
3½oz (100g) plain flour

Magic Sauce:
3½oz (100g) butter
4 tablespoons sugar
2 teaspoons grated orange rind
8 tablespoons orange juice
1 teaspoon lemon juice
4 tablespoons orange-flavoured liqueur
2 tablespoons brandy

Light and delicious tofu crêpes in a luscious, flaming sauce are sure to add drama to any occasion.

To prepare the dessert, mix all the batter ingredients in a blender until smooth. Cook them according to the

A delicious dish for a candlelit dinner Tofu crêpes enflamed with liqueur and brandy are perfect romantic fare.

instructions for pancakes (see below).

For the sauce, cream the butter and sugar together and add the orange rind, orange juice and lemon juice. Heat the mixture in a frying pan or chafing dish. Dip the tofu crêpes into the sauce, fold them in quarters and gently edge to the sides of the pan. For the final flaming effect, heat the liqueur and brandy in a small pan, pour this over the crêpes and ignite.

PANCAKES

1 egg
7oz (198g) mashed tofu
2.8fl oz (80ml) milk
1 tablespoon salad oil
1 tablespoon sugar

½ teaspoon vanilla essence
½ teaspoon baking powder
¼ teaspoon salt
3½oz (100g) plain flour

For this tasty recipe, which combined a traditional pancake mix with protein-rich tofu, combine all the ingredients in a blender until smooth. Lightly grease a frying pan and heat until fairly hot. Pour about four tablespoons of the pancake batter into the pan and cook on both sides until golden brown. Repeat with the rest of the batter, taking care that the cooked pancakes are kept covered and hot. Serve with whatever topping you like – sugar and lemon juice, butter, jam, or fresh fruit.

SOFT SPICE COOKIES

1 egg
7oz (198g) mashed tofu
5oz (142g) brown sugar
8 tablespoons salad oil
1 teaspoon ginger
1 teaspoon cinnamon
1 teaspoon vanilla essence
½ teaspoon nutmeg
½ teaspoon salt
8¾oz (250g) plain flour
½ teaspoon bicarbonate of
   soda
5oz (142g) chopped dried fruits
4¼ (120g) whole mixed nuts

These tasty tofu-enriched cookies make a nutritious alernative to regular biscuits.

To prepare, mix together the first nine ingredients in a blender until smooth and set aside. Sift together the flour and bicarbonate in a large bowl and add the tofu mixture to form a sticky dough. Arrange teaspoonfuls of the dough on greased baking sheet. To decorate, press a nut onto each cookie.

Preheat the oven and bake the cookies at 350°F (180°C) for about ten minutes or until they are golden brown around the edges. Cool on a wire rack.

As an artistic variation, omit the dried fruit and pipe the dough in circles. Cook as above. String ribbon or coloured braid through the cookies and hang them for a festive occasion.

HOLIDAY FRUIT CAKE

10oz (283g) plain flour
1½ teaspoons bicarbonate of
   soda
1 egg
8 tablespoons salad oil
7oz (198g) mashed tofu
16 tablespoons brown sugar

2 teaspoons cinnamon
½ teaspooon salt
1 teaspoon brandy
5½oz (160g) mixed dried fruit
4½oz (130g) chopped nuts
8 tablespoons apricot jam for
   glaze (optional)

Delicious as traditional Christmas fare, this tofu fruitcake is much lower in calories and makes a highly nutritious tea-time treat.

To prepare, mix together the flour and bicarbonate in a large bowl. Combine the egg, oil, tofu, sugar and brandy together in a blender until smooth. Add the mixture, little by little, to the flour, stirring until well combined. Mix in the fruit and nuts. Fill a quart-sized ring mould with the cake mixture and bake at 350°F (180°C) for about 35 minutes or until a skewer inserted in the centre of the cake comes out clean. Cool, wrap well and store in the refrigerator. Before serving, melt the jam with a little water in a small saucepan and brush this over the surface of the cake.

To make buns, using the same recipe, spoon the mixture into patty tins and bake for 20 minutes.

SWEET POTATO PIE

1 prepared 9in (23cm) pie shell (p.103)	¾ cup (150g) brown sugar
	2 eggs
2 cups (400g) cooked sweet potatoes, mashed	1 strip orange peel
	½ teaspoon salt
1lb (450g) tofu	¼ teaspoon nutmeg
1 cup (240ml) fresh orange juice	1 tablespoon cornflour
½ cup (126g) butter or margarine	1 teaspoon vanilla essence

The unusual combination of tofu, sweet potatoes and spices make this a delightfully different dessert.

To prepare, first prebake the pie shell for five minutes at 350°F (180°C) and set aside. Combine the potatoes, tofu, juice, butter, sugar, eggs, orange peel, salt, nutmeg, cornflour and vanilla in a blender until smooth. Pour the tofu mixture into the cooked pie shell and bake for about 35-40 minutes, or until a knife inserted in the centre of the pie comes out clean.

Chill the pie thoroughly before serving.

Two delicious confections Holiday Fruitcake – much lower in calories than traditional fruitcakes – and Sweet Potato Pie, an unusual spicy orange pie.

VANILLA COFFEE BAVARIAN CREAM

An exotic cream and coffee creation This delicate sweet is sure to please.

10oz (283g) tofu
3 tablespoons powdered
  gelatine
4 egg yolks
16 tablespoons sugar

1 pint (½l) milk
½ teaspoon vanilla essence
7fl oz (198ml) double cream
1 tablespoon instant coffee

To prepare this decorative sweet, first wrap the tofu in a cloth and allow to stand for 30 minutes. Meanwhile, soak the gelatine in ¼ pint (142ml) cold water. Next, purée the tofu in a blender until smooth. In a saucepan, beat the

egg yolks and sugar until creamy. Add the milk and cook over a low heat until thickened, stirring constantly with a wooden spoon to avoid scorching. Add the vanilla and soaked gelatine. Stir until all the gelatine is completely dissolved, taking care not to boil. Add the tofu purée and mix well.

To cool the mixture, place the saucepan in a large bowl filled with iced water. The water should reach a level half the height of the saucepan. Stir until the mixture begins to thicken but do not allow it to set. Whip the double cream until stiff and lightly fold it into the mixture. Rinse a 1½ quart pudding mould with cold water and fill three quarters full with the cream mixture. Mix the coffee, dissolved in one tablespoon hot water, with the remaining cream. Then pour this into an icing bag with a 2in (5cm) round nozzle. Insert the nozzle in the centre of the vanilla cream and pipe slowly until all the coffee cream is used. The vanilla cream will move automatically to the wall of the mould leaving the coffee cream in the centre. Carefully remove the nozzle to ensure that the none of the coffee cream comes out.

Finally, chill the mixture. Turn out and serve.

COCONUT TOFU DESSERT

10oz (283g) tofu
1 pint (½l) milk
7oz (198g) coconut flakes
8 tablespoons sugar
4 tablespoons powdered
    gelatine, soaked in ¼
    pint (142ml) water

½ teaspoon vanilla essence

For Brown Sugar Syrup:
6oz (170g) brown sugar
7oz (198g) white sugar
½ pint (¼l) water
1 egg white

For this coconut dessert with its delicious syrup topping, first bring the milk to a boil in a saucepan. Remove from the heat and add the coconut. Allow the mixture to stand for ten minutes as the milk absorbs the coconut flavouring. Then pour the liquid through a sieve into another saucepan and press well. Add the sugar and soaked gelatine to the coconut milk and heat gently, without boiling, until the sugar and gelatine dissolve. Next, purée the tofu in a blender. Pour it into the gelatine mixture. Stir in the vanilla essence. Rinse a pudding mould 5in x 4in x 3in (12cm x 10cm x 7cm) with cold water. Pour in the tofu gelatine mixture and chill.

For the topping, mix the brown sugar, water and egg white in a saucepan. Bring to the boil. Immediately reduce the heat and cook slowly until the egg white foam becomes transparent. Strain through a cloth and chill. Pour over the dessert and serve.

TOFU CINNAMON BUNS

1lb (453g) tofu
5¼oz (149g) butter
1 teaspoon salt
10½oz (298g) plain flour
2 teaspoons baking powder

2½oz (70g) brown sugar
1 teaspoon cinnamon
8 tablespoons chopped nuts
2 tablespoons butter or
  margarine

Spicy cinnamon buns, served as a dessert or teatime treat are child's play to prepare.

First mix the tofu, the main quantity of the butter and salt in a blender until smooth. Set aside. Combine the flour and baking powder in a bowl. Add the tofu mixture and stir well together. The dough should be soft and somewhat sticky. Next, mix the brown sugar, cinnamon and nuts and set aside. On a floured surface, roll out the tofu dough to form a rectangle about ¾in (19mm) thick. Spread two tablespoons of butter on the surface of the dough and sprinkle with the cinnamon-sugar mixture. Roll up the rectangle and cut into slices about 1in (2.5cm) thick. Place the buns cut side down on a greased baking sheet, so that the sides of the buns barely touch.

Preheat an oven to 350°F (180°C) and bake for about 30 minutes or until the buns are light brown and no longer doughy. Serve immediately or reheat before serving.

A spicy tea-time treat
Cinnamon buns should be served piping hot and like the proverbial hot cakes, they will disappear.

TOFU MANGO DESSERT

7oz (198g) mashed tofu
2 mangoes, about 1lb (453g)
Juice of 1 lemon
7fl oz (199ml) double cream
1 egg yolk

3 tablespoons powdered
  gelatine
½ pint (¼l) water
4¼ (120g) sugar

To prepare mangoes in a delicious tofu cream whip, first peel the fruit, remove the stone and finely dice the flesh. Combine the mango, tofu and egg yolk in a blender, and set aside. Soak the gelatine in three tablespoons of cold water. Mix the water and sugar in a saucepan. Heat, without boiling, until the sugar is dissolved. Pour into a bowl. Add the lemon juice, tofu-mango mixture and stir until blended. Chill.

Meanwhile, whip the cream. When the gelatine mixture begins to thicken, fold in the whipped cream. Rinse six small moulds or one quart mould with cold water. Fill with the mango mixture and chill. To serve, decorate with mango slices.

Delicious desserts These refreshing desserts make the perfect ending to a meal.
From top: Tofu Mango Dessert and Tofu Lemon Desert with Raspberry Sauce.

TOFU LEMON DESSERT

1 lemon
7oz (198g) mashed tofu
3 tablespoons (27g) gelatine,
  soaked in 3 tablespoons
  water
12 tablespoons sugar

11fl oz (312ml) water
Juice of 1½ lemons
1 egg white

For garnish:
Raspberry sauce

To prepare this refreshing dessert, first chill six individual moulds. Next, peel the lemon, slice thinly and set aside. In a saucepan, combine the water and sugar. Heat until the sugar has dissolved. Add the soaked gelatine and dissolve, without boiling, over a low heat. Add the lemon juice, mix and allow to cool.

Fill the first mould with the gelatine and leave it to chill in the refrigerator until a film of gelatine has coated the wall and base. Pour the excess gelatine back into the saucepan. Lay a slice of lemon on the base of the mould and repeat the process with the other five. When all are coated, mix the tofu and the remaining gelatine in a bowl and chill until the mixture thickens. Beat the egg white and fold it into the mixture. Pour into the gelatine-coated moulds and chill.

For the raspberry sauce, purée 7oz (198g) of ripe rapsberries. Add 8 tablespoons of sugar and 4 tablespoons of Cointreau. Mix well until the sugar has dissolved. Strain. Turn out the moulds and decorate with the sauce.

TOFU WHITE CHOCOLATE CREAM

6oz (170g) mashed tofu
¼ pint (⅛l) milk
2¼ teaspoons (5g) powdered gelatine, dissolved in a tablespoon of water
3½oz (99g) white chocolate

2 tablespoons honey (less if chocolate is very sweet)
A pinch of cardamon, mace and cinnamon
Sliced, toasted almonds as garnish

This exquisite tofu dessert is a perfect finale to any candlelit dinner or other very special occasion. It can be prepared in advance but must be kept cool.

First, wrap the tofu in a cloth and allow to stand for 15 minutes. Then blend until smooth and set aside. Warm the milk and dissolve the gelatine in it. Do not allow to boil. Set aside. Use a double boiler to melt the white chocolate. Add the milk, chocolate, honey and spices to the tofu purée and blend again. Allow to cool. Spoon the mixture into individual glasses and chill. Garnish with toasted almond slices and the sweet is ready to serve.

BANANA CREAM PIE

1 tablespoon (9g) gelatine
6 tablespoons water
10oz (283g) mashed tofu
1 egg
4 tablespoons sugar

Juice of 1 lemon
⅛ teaspoon salt
2 large bananas
1 crumb crust pie shell (p.102)

To prepare this delicious summer pie, soak the gelatine first in three tablespoons of water for five minutes. Add three more tablespoons of water and heat gently over a low heat until dissolved, taking care not to boil the solution. Mix the remaining six ingredients together in a blender until smooth. Add the melted gelatine and blend until well mixed. Pour the filling into the crumb crust and chill for at least four hours, or overnight. Just before serving, decorate with slices of banana and swirls of Tofu Whip (p.102).

EASY-TO-DO TOFU CHEESECAKE

3½oz (100g) sugar
7oz (198g) butter
10½oz (298g) plain flour
10½oz (298g) pressed tofu
1 can (397g) sweetened

condensed milk
4 eggs, separated
2 tablespoons cornflour
¼ teaspoon lemon essence
Juice of 2 lemons

As the name suggests, the preparation of this nutritious

Simply special Easy-to-Do
Cheesecake is child's play to
prepare.

dessert presents no problems. As a variation, try omitting the crust to create a delicious soufflé.

Begin by preheating the oven to 375°F (190°C). Grease the base of a 10in (24cm) Springform baking tin, dust with flour and set aside. Next, mix the sugar, butter and flour together in a bowl. Spread the dough over the base of the baking tin and press lightly. In a blender, mix together all the ingredients for the filling except the egg whites until the mixture is quite smooth. Beat the egg whites until stiff. Pour the tofu mixture over the egg white and mix gently with a plastic spatula. Pour the filling over the crust and bake on the lowest shelf of the oven for about 60-70 minutes.

Allow to cool in the pan. Take out and serve.

DESSERTS AND CAKES

TOFU WHIP

12¼oz (347g) drained tofu
¼ teaspoon salt
3 tablespoons sugar

1 teaspoon vanilla essence
1 tablespoon salad oil

This is a glorious way to top a pie or cold dessert.

To prepare, simply mix together all the ingredients in a blender until smooth. Use exactly as you would whipped cream and keep any surplus whip covered in the refrigerator.

SOY WHIP

3 tablespoons rich soymilk (see p.20)
6 tablespoons salad oil

1 tablespoon sugar
A pinch of salt
½ teaspoon vanilla essence

This versatile whipped topping can be prepared with either homemade or purchased soymilk. The consistency can be varied to make the whip soft or firm, by adjusting the amount of oil added.

To prepare, mix the soymilk, three tablespoons of the oil, sugar, salt and vanilla together in a blender until smooth. Continue blending at a low speed and add the oil slowly in a thin stream until the whip has reached the desired consistency. More oil will produce a thicker whip. Soy whip can be served, just like real cream, with a variety of desserts. This recipe will make about half a cup of topping.

CRUMB CRUST

4 tablespoons wheat germ
3½ oz (100g) dry
　　breadcrumbs
4 tablespoons brown sugar
1 teaspoon cinnamon
2 tablespoons salad oil
3 tablespoons butter or
　　margarine

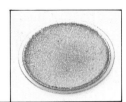

To prepare this delicious crust which makes a perfect spicy base for sweets such as Refrigerator Cheesecake (p.91), mix all the ingredients together by hand until blended. Press the crumb mixture into a 9in pie dish. If a thin crust is required three quarters of the mixture will probably suffice. The surplus can be used as a topping. Bake the shell for five minutes at 325°F (160°C).

Cool before filling.

SHORT CRUST

8¾oz (248g) flour
4¼oz (120g) butter
1 egg
A pinch of salt
2 tablespoons cold water

This recipe makes a good basic pastry that can be used for a variety of sweet and savoury dishes. To prepare, sift the flour in a bowl. Add the butter, egg and salt blending them quickly into the flour. Add the water little by little and form the dough to a ball. Chill for two hours. Press the dough directly into the pie dish or roll it out first between two pieces of wax paper. Bake the crust in a fairly hot oven 400°F (200°C) or as the recipe directs.

GINGERBREAD COOKIES

8¾oz (248g) brown sugar
7oz (198g) mashed tofu
8 tablespoons salad oil
8 tablespoons treacle
2 teaspoons ginger
2 teaspoons cinnamon
¼ teaspoon cloves
¼ teaspoon nutmeg
1 teaspoon salt
2 teaspoons bicarbonate of soda
27-29oz (770-840g) plain flour

Gingerbread cookies make gingerbread men or any variety of shapes you can choose to delight your family or create an interesting tea-time party spread.

To prepare, mix the brown sugar, tofu, oil, treacle, spices, salt and bicarbonate together in a blender until smooth. Set aside. In a large bowl, mix the flour and tofu mixture, kneading it as it becomes thicker. Chill the dough for three hours or overnight. When well-chilled, place it between two sheets of waxed paper and roll out to a thickness of ⅛-¼in (3-8mm). Cut the dough into the shapes required. Preheat the oven to 350°F (180°C) and bake the cookies for about eight minutes or until firm and slightly brown around the edges. The biscuits will keep in an air-tight container for about a month.

Exquisite desserts for an elegant occasion Tofu White Chocolate Pudding and Banana Cream Pie are as delicious as they are pleasing to the eye.

Tofu By-Products – Okara, Agé And Yuba
Okara Crackers * Okaraola * Okara Cutlets * Okara
Marrow Pie And Tarts * Hot Okara Wrapped In Lettuce *
Chicken With Okara Stuffing * Okara Bonbons * Okara
Fruit Tart * Steamed Chestnut Okara Pudding * Okara
Lemon Cake * Okara Carrot Cake * Chocolate Chip
Cookies * Thin Okara Cookies * Okara Honey Cookies *
Oatmeal Okara Cookies * Okara Banana Bread * Okara
Blueberry Muffins * Okara Crêpes * Agé Risotto * Grilled
Agé * Surprise Agé Pouches * Steamed Yuba Rolls *
Stuffed Fried Yuba Rolls

TOFU BY-PRODUCTS
OKARA, AGE, AND YUBA

Okara, agé and yuba, which are all relatively novel ingredients in the West, can be employed in a number of delicious ways. Okara, the soybean pulp obtained during tofu-making, is rich in fibre and protein and has a delicious nutty flavour. The following recipes show how to use it in appetizers, main meals and sweets.

Agé, deep-fried slices of tofu, makes a delicious addition to risotto; it can also be stuffed with a variety of tasty fillings. Yuba, perhaps the most unusual soybean by-product, is prepared by skimming the surface of boiling soymilk and draining and drying the skin. In two recipes included here, thin sheets of yuba are stuffed, rolled, steamed or deep-fried.

Preparing such dishes demands some time and care, but will also give you enormous satisfaction, as you delight family and friends alike with a truly exotic meal.

OKARA CRACKERS

6oz (175g) okara
5oz (141g) whole wheat flour
2½oz (70g) wheat germ

1 teaspoon salt
8 tablespoons salad oil
3 tablespoons mashed tofu

Savoury Okara Crackers are a delicious accompaniment to an apéritif or cocktail. They can be created in a wide variety of flavours, according to taste. Try adding half a teaspoon of curry, or a quarter cup of grated Parmesan cheese, shredded coconut or sesame, caraway or poppy seeds to the dough.

To prepare, mix all the ingredients together in a bowl. Knead the dough for about five minutes until smooth. Roll out the dough between two sheets of wax paper until it is ⅛in (3mm) thick. Then, cut the dough into different shapes using biscuit cutters; this recipe should make about sixty biscuits.

Place the crackers on baking sheets, taking care to leave some space between each cracker, and bake at 325°F (160°C) for about ten minutes or until the crackers are light brown and crisp.

Cool and store in an airtight container.

OKARAOLA

8½oz (240g) oatmeal
2½oz (70g) wheat germ
8 tablespoons toasted sesame
  seeds
4½oz (130g) sliced almonds
11½oz (325g) okara

2 tablespoons cinnamon
6fl oz (170ml) water
8oz (226g) honey
5.7fl oz (162ml) salad oil
16 tablespoons raisins

Okaraola served with yoghurt, or milk and fruit, is a delicious and healthy way to start the day.

For its preparation, mix together the oatmeal, wheat germ, sesame seeds, almonds, okara and cinnamon in a large bowl. Set aside.

Mix the water, salad oil and honey in a saucepan and heat until they blend together. Pour the hot honey solution over the okara mixture, stirring until all the dry ingredients are moist. Spread the cereal on two large baking sheets and bake at 325°F (160°C) for about 25 minutes. Stir every 10 minutes until the mixture is dry and light brown in colour. Cool, then stir in the raisins.

To store the cereal, pack in airtight containers. And remember that this cereal is extremely filling. An average-sized breakfast serving should be no more than four heaped tablespoons – unless you are really hungry!

Breakfast treat
Okaraola, served with yoghurt, fruit and milk and accompanied by a dish of okara crackers, makes a delicious start to the day.

OKARA CUTLETS

6½oz (185g) okara
3½oz (100g) flour
¼ teaspoon dry mustard
2 tablespoons soy sauce
¼ teaspoon sage

¼ teaspoon oregano
½ teaspoon salt
4 tablespoons chopped onion
1 egg
16 tablespoons breadcrumbs

Spicy Okara Cutlets are simple to prepare and are gourmet vegetarian fare. They should be served piping hot straight from the stove with a tangy mix of Worcester sauce and tomato ketchup to complement their taste.

Begin by mixing together all the ingredients except the breadcrumbs. Shape the mixture into four cutlets. Coat each with the breadcrumbs. Heat a little oil in a frying pan and cook the cutlets until the centres are firm and they are brown on each side.

Serve with salad or a fresh vegetable.

Gourmet vegetarian fare
Rich in protein and spicy, delicious Okara Cutlets are quick and inexpensive to prepare.

OKARA MARROW PIE AND TARTS

For filling:
16 tablespoons breadcrumbs
½ pint (¼l) milk
2oz (56g) marrow
2½oz (70g) okara
Salt, pepper and nutmeg
1 egg

For crust:
8¾oz (250g) flour
4½oz 127g) butter
1 small egg or 1 egg white
2 tablespoons cold water
A pinch of salt

A savoury specialty Golden-brown Okara Marrow Pie and Tarts should be served piping hot as a snack or main meal.

Tasty marrow and okara in a golden brown pastry crust make decorative and delicious supper fare. Serve hot with a glass of red wine to create an occasion.

To prepare, mix together all the crust ingredients except the water. Add the water little by little to form a smooth dough. Wrap the dough in foil and chill in the refrigerator for at least two hours.

For the filling, grate the marrow into a bowl and set aside. Soak the breadcrumbs in the milk, then press and squeeze out the moisture. Add the breadcrumbs, okara, egg and seasonings to the marrow and knead to form a smooth dough. Set aside.

Butter a pie dish or smaller brioche or tartlet moulds; this recipe makes about five tarts in 3½in. (8.5cm) moulds or eight tarts in 2½in moulds. Roll out the pastry dough to a thickness of ⅕in (5mm). Line the pie dish or moulds with the dough and fill with the okara-marrow mixture. Cover with the remaining dough and trim off the excess pastry around the edges. Finally, brush the surface with beaten egg yolk and bake in a moderate oven for 25-30 minutes. Serve hot.

OKARA, AGE, YUBA

HOT OKARA WRAPPED IN LETTUCE

8 tablespoons minced shitake
   (black Japanese mushrooms)
8 tablespoons minced carrot
8 tablespoons minced celery
½ medium onion, minced
8 tablespoons minced pine nuts
   or walnuts

4 tablespoons sesame oil
10½oz (300g) okara
3 tablespoons shoyu (soy) sauce
3 tablespoons sake
1 tablespoon chilli powder (or
   according to taste)
8-12 firm lettuce leaves

This unusual spicy, oriental fare, served on lettuce leaves, is sure to surprise and delight. This recipe is hot but the spices can be varied according to taste and imagination.

To prepare, first heat the sesame oil in a frying pan. Sauté the vegetables and pine nuts for five minutes. Add the okara and continue to sauté. Add the seasonings and sauté for another five minutes. Remove from the heat. Wash and drain the lettuce leaves and pat dry with a cloth.

Present the lettuce leaves on a platter with the bowl of okara and vegetables beside it. Each guest should then be served one or two lettuce leaves with two tablespoonfuls of the okara mixture to each leaf.

Wrap the hot okara in lettuce leaves. It can then be eaten held in the fingers.

Deliciously different Hot Okara Wrapped in Lettuce Leaves is an interesting way to entertain your friends.

CHICKEN WITH OKARA STUFFING

1 2lb (0.9kg) chicken
2 teaspoons salt
1 teaspoon sugar
½ teaspoon paprika
5oz (141g) okara
1 egg
1 teaspoon thyme

3 tablespoons each of finely
   chopped parsley, celery,
   onion
½ teaspoon pepper
A pinch each of powdered
   cloves and cardamom
½ teaspoon salt
2 tablespoons brandy

Spices, herbs and okara in an unusual stuffing make this chicken quite an exotic bird.

To prepare, combine the salt, sugar and paprika. Rub the chicken inside and out with the mixture. Set aside. Mix together all the other ingredients in a bowl. Stuff the chicken with the mixture. Close the opening with kitchen twine or skewers. Brush the chicken with oil.

To cook, preheat an oven to a moderate heat and roast the chicken for about one hour. Test that it is cooked by inserting a skewer. The juices should run clear.

This chicken dish is delicious hot with fresh cooked vegetables or cold with a salad or as picnic fare.

OKARA BONBONS

8 tablespoons peanut butter
2½oz (70g) okara (if uncooked, heat for 15 minutes stirring constantly. Cool before use.
3 tablespoons honey

4 tablespoons milk powder
1 tablespoon cocoa, coconut, chopped nuts or wheat germ for rolling

These rich, nutty bonbons are a perfect way to finish an elegant meal. Dip them in melted chocolate for an extra luscious touch.

To prepare, mix together the peanut butter, okara, honey and skim milk powder. The dough should be stiff enough to roll into balls. More milk powder can be added if the mixture is sticky. Divide the dough in two and mix one half with the cocoa. Break off pieces of the dough of each flavour and roll each piece into a 1in (2.5cm) diameter ball.

For the final touch, roll the bonbons in cocoa, wheat germ, coconut or chopped nuts and they are ready to serve.

OKARA FRUIT TART

For crust:
4 tablespoons sugar
3½oz (100g) butter
5¼oz (150g) plain flour

For topping:
16 tablespoons stewed fruit

5¼oz (125g) unsalted butter
8 tablespoons sugar
2 eggs
16 tablespoons okara
½ teaspoon rum essence

The distinctive nutty flavour of okara makes this an unusual and exotic dessert or tea-time treat.

To prepare, first mix together all the ingredients for the crust, by hand or using a pastry blender. Grease an 8in (20cm) flan dish and dust with flour. Press the dough over the base of the dish and bake in a preheated oven at 375°F (190°C) for 15 minutes. Remove the dish from the oven, allow the crust to cool for five minutes and then spread the drained fruit over it. Set the dish aside.

For the topping, cream the butter and sugar together. Add the eggs one by one and mix well. Loosen the okara and add it to the egg mixture. Finally blend in the rum essence and pour the mixture over the fruit. Bake the tart in a preheated oven at 375°F (190°C) for 30 minutes or until a skewer inserted in the centre of the topping comes out clean. Cool and unmould the tart.

Lastly, if desired, prepare a glaze. Warm half a cup of apricot jam mixed with two tablespoons of water over a low heat and brush over the surface of the tart.

An autumn dessert
Chestnuts and nutty-
flavoured okara are
combined with hot
chocolate sauce in this tasty
sweet.

STEAMED CHESTNUT OKARA PUDDING

10½oz (300g) chestnuts,
  peeled cooked and drained
4 eggs
½ teaspoon salt
4 tablespoons chestnut syrup

4 tablespoons salad oil
½ teaspoon vanilla extract
2 teaspoons baking powder
7oz (198g) okara

To prepare this delicious dessert, first peel the chestnuts. Bring ½ pint (240ml) water and eight tablespoons of sugar to the boil. Add the peeled chestnuts and cook until soft. Cool and retain the syrup. Dice one third of the chestnuts and set aside. Purée the rest of the chestnuts in a blender. Add the eggs, salt, chestnut syrup, oil and vanilla, blending until the mixture is smooth. Set aside. Mix the okara and baking powder together in a bowl, stir in the chestnut mixture and add the diced chestnuts.

Grease a single large mould or eight individual ones and pour in the mixture. Steam at a high temperature for around 45 minutes or until the centre is spring to the touch. Turn out and serve with chocolate sauce.

OKARA LEMON CAKE

6 egg yolks
8 tablespoons brown sugar
8 tablespoons white sugar
½ teaspoon vanilla essence
8½oz (240g) okara
2½oz (70g) plain flour

1 teaspoon baking powder
Juice of ½ lemon
6 egg whites
4½oz (130g) icing sugar
2 tablespoons lemon juice

To prepare this light, tangy tea-time treat, first grease a 10in (25cm) spring-release tin and dust lightly with flour. Beat the egg yolks with the brown sugar until creamy. Add the vanilla essence and lemon juice and mix until smooth. Sift the flour and baking powder into the egg yolk mixture, mixing well. Crumble the okara until it is free of lumps and add this to the mixture. Set aside

Beat the egg whites with the white sugar until very stiff. Fold the egg whites little by little into the egg yolk-okara mixture. Fill the spring-release tin with the mixture and bake in an oven pre-heated to 375° (190°C) for 45 minutes. Turn out and cool.

For the topping, mix the icing sugar with the lemon juice and spread over the surface of the cake. Decorate with slices of candied lemon, if desired.

OKARA CARROT CAKE

6 eggs, separated
6oz (170g) brown sugar
3¼oz (92g) white sugar
2½oz (70g) flour
A pinch of cinnamon
A pinch of cloves

A pinch of salt
1 teaspoon baking powder
2 tablespoons Kirschwasser
3 finely grated carrots
8½oz (240g) okara

To prepare this rich, spicy cake, first preheat the oven to 375°F (190°C). Beat the egg yolks and brown sugar together until creamy and set aside. Sift together the flour, spices, salt and baking powder and add them to the egg yolk mixture. Stir well. Blend in the kirschwasser. Make sure the okara is dry. and crumble it until it is free of lumps. Add the okara and the carrots to the egg yolk mixture. Beat the egg whites and white sugar together until stiff. Gently fold them, little by little, into the okara mixture. Set aside.

Grease and flour the base of a sring-release tin. Pour in the batter, smoothing over the surface with a spatula and bake for about 40 minutes, or until a skewer pressed into the centre of the cake comes out clean. Turn out and cool on a cake rack. When the cake is cold, frost the surface with melted chocolate and allow to harden.

CHOCOLATE CHIP COOKIES

7oz (198g) margarine
3¼oz (92g) sugar
1 egg
1 teaspoon vanilla essence
5oz (141g) flour

½ teaspoon bicarbonate of soda
½ teaspoon salt (optional)
7oz (198g) okara
6oz (170g) semi-sweet
    chocolate chips

To prepare these crisply delicious Chocolate Chip Cookies, mix together the margarine, sugar, egg and vanilla in a bowl. Sift together the flour, soda and salt and stir this into the margarine/egg mixture. Stir in the okara, mixing until smooth. Then add the chocolate chips and mix again.

Drop teaspoonfuls of the mixture about 1in (3cm) apart on an ungreased baking sheet. Bake the cookies at 400°F (200°C) for about 10 minutes or until lightly browned. At this stage the cookies should be soft. Cool slightly before removing them from the baking sheet. They will harden as they cool. When they are quite cold, transfer them to an air-tight tin and store until required.

THIN OKARA COOKIES

1 teaspoon vanilla essence
7oz (198g) flour
3½oz (100g) dried okara

1 egg
5¼oz (150g) butter
3¼ oz (92g) sugar '

A sweet selection
Decorative
okara biscuits you will be
proud to serve.

These thin, elegant cookies complement a coffee party and add sophistication to a tea-time spread.

To prepare, first dry the okara. This is done by heating it slowly in a large frying pan or wok. To avoid burning, stir constantly with a wooden spoon for twenty to thirty minutes or until it becomes light and fluffy. To achieve the fine grain required in this recipe, sift the okara through a metal colander. Set aside.

In a bowl, blend together the egg, butter, sugar and vanilla essence. Add the flour and okara, mixing well. Roll out to form a thin sheet about 1/10in (2.5mm) thick. Cut into 2in (5cm) squares. Lay these carefully on a well-greased baking sheet and bake at 375°F (190°C) for about ten minutes or until golden brown.

To retain crispness, store in an air-tight container.

OKARA HONEY COOKIES

1¾oz (50g) butter	2 tablespoons double cream
1¾oz (50g) sugar	Grated rind of ½ lemon
2 tablespoons honey	3½oz (100g) dried okara

To prepare these delicious nutty-flavoured cookies, first dry the okara by heating it gently in a large frying pan for twenty to thirty minutes, stirring constantly. Mix together the butter, sugar, honey, cream and lemon rind. Stir in the okara and blend until smooth. Shape the biscuits by first rolling the dough into small balls and then flattening them out. Set the cookies about 2in (5cm) apart on a greased baking sheet. Bake at 350°F (180°C) for about 20 minutes or until golden brown.

OATMEAL OKARA COOKIES

5.8fl oz (165ml) salad oil	1 teaspoon cinnamon
1 egg	1 teaspoon vanilla essence
4oz (113g) brown sugar	5oz (141g) plain flour
2½oz (70g) okara	4½oz (130g) oatmeal
½ teaspoon salt	2½oz (70g) chopped almonds
½ teaspoon baking powder	

These rich, spicy cookies are easy to prepare. Simply mix together all the ingredients in a large bowl to form a soft dough. Roll the dough into 1in (2.5cm) balls and place on a greased baking sheet allowing 1½in (3.5cm) between the balls. Flatten and shape the cookies and sprinkle with sugar. Bake at 350°F (180°C) for 10 minutes.

OKARA BANANA BREAD

1 egg
2½oz (70g) okara
1 teaspoon baking powder
½ teaspoon bicarbonate of soda
7¼oz (212g) plain flour
5oz (141g) chopped nuts
1 teaspoon grated orange rind

8 tablespoons brown sugar
8 tablespoons salad oil
4 tablespoons orange juice
3 small bananas
½ teaspoon salt
1 teaspoon vanilla essence

Delicious Okara Banana Bread is tasty and healthy tea-time fare.

To prepare, mix together the first seven ingredients in a blender until smooth. Pour the mixture into a large bowl. Stir in the remaining ingredients to form a thick batter. Pour the batter into the greased loaf pan and bake at 325°F (160°C) for about 45 minutes or until a skewer inserted in the centre comes out clean.

Cool the bread in the pan for 30 minutes and then turn out onto a cake rack.

OKARA BLUEBERRY MUFFINS

1 egg
4 tablespoons sugar
½ teaspoon salt
½ pint (¼l) milk
4 tablespoons salad oil
½ teaspoon vanilla essence

3½oz (100g) flour
1 tablespoon baking powder
4¼oz (120g) cornmeal
5oz (141g) okara
8¼oz (240g) bilberries

Okara gives muffins a delicious nutty flavour, which blends well with the tart fruit taste of blueberries. To prepare, first grease 12 deep patty tins. Sift the flour and baking powder together and set aside. Loosen the okara and stir it into the cornmeal, mixing until all lumps have disappeared. Add this to the flour mixture. Set aside.

Mix the first six ingredients together in a bowl. Add these to the flour mixture and mix until just combined. Fold in the blueberries. Fill the patty tins until ⅔ full. Bake in a preheated oven at 375°F (190°C) for 30 minutes or until a skewer inserted in the centre comes out clean and the muffins are light brown. Serve hot with butter.

OKARA CREPES

2 eggs
12.6fl oz (329ml) milk
2½oz (70g) okara
3½oz (100g) plain flour

½ teaspoon salt
2 teaspoons sugar
2 tablespoons salad oil

These luscious crêpes are delicately flavoured with the nutty taste of okara. To prepare, mix all the ingredients together in a blender until smooth. Allow the batter to stand for one hour. If it seems too thick, a little extra milk can be added.

Using a small frying pan or crêpe pan, heat a little oil until it is hot. Pour a small amount of batter into the pan and rotate it until the batter covers the base of the pan. Cook the crêpe until the bottom is light brown. Loosen the edges of the crêpe with a spatula and flip it over to brown the other side. Stack the cooked crêpes with wax paper between them to prevent sticking and keep them in a warm place, covered.

Serve the crêpes hot with jam, honey or ice-cream. If, however, the occasion demands something more dramatic, follow the recipe for Magic Sauce (p.92) and serve the crêpes flaming.

AGE RISOTTO

A fish and rice dish enhanced by agé This exotic risotto makes a delicious lunch or evening meal.

10½oz (300g) rice
20fl oz (568ml) water
2 tablespoons vegetable oil
4 pieces agé (2in x 4in, 5cm x 10cm)

8 tablespoons minced onion
2½lb (1.1kg) salmon fillet
7oz (198g) green peas
5¼oz (150g) sliced mushrooms

To prepare this unusual fish dish, first wash the rice and drain well in a colander. Sauté the onion in oil and then add the rice and sauté for a further five minutes or until the rice becomes translucent. Add the water, agé, salmon, peas and mushrooms, seasoning to taste with salt and pepper. Bring the mixture to a boil and cook over a high heat for five minutes. Reduce the heat and cook covered for 15 minutes or until the rice is cooked.

GRILLED AGE

4 pieces agé (2in x 4in, 5cm x 10cm each)
2 tablespoons red miso (soybean paste)

1 tablespoon sugar
2 tablespoons minced spring onion

Grilled agé is very simple to make and serves as an excellent hors d'oeuvre. Red miso, another soybean by-product is available from specialty and health stores. To prepare, first form the pouches from the agé by slitting the longest edge with a sharp knife. Set aside. In a small bowl, combine the miso, sugar and onion. Mix well and divide into four portions. Fill each of the agé pouches evenly with a knife spread. Grill or sauté the stuffed pouches until brown and crisp. Cut into bite-sized pieces and serve.

SURPRISE AGE POUCHES

8 pieces agé (about 1½in x 5in, 4cm x 12.5cm)
½ carrot, cut into matchsticks
½ celery stalk, cut into matchsticks
A handful of spinach leaves, parboiled
2 strips of bacon, chopped

4 eggs
2 potatoes, grated and drained
8 gingko nuts (available from Chinese or Japanese speciality stores, parboiled, peeled
¾ pint (375ml) water
1 chicken stock cube

To prepare this delicious dish, cut the agé and pull apart to form 16 pouches. Fill four of the pouches with carrots and celery and the next four with spinach and bacon. Stuff a further four with potato and gingko nuts and drop an egg into the last four pouches. Tie the opening of each with a string or fasten with a small skewer or toothpick.

For the next step, mix the water and stock cube in a large saucepan and bring to the boil. If possible, lay the agé pouches in one layer in the broth and cook over a medium heat for ten minutes. To serve, arrange the pouches on a large dish and accompany with cooked rice.

STEAMED YUBA ROLLS

8 sheets dried yuba (5in x 4in, 12.5cm x 10cm)
10½oz (300g) tofu
7oz (198g) minced pork
8 tablespoons minced shiitake (black Japanese mushrooms. These should be soaked in lukewarm water for 30 minutes to reconstitute) or use regular mushrooms
3 tablespoons minced spring onions
1 tablespoon grated ginger root
½ teaspoon salt
1 teaspoon shoyu (soy) sauce
½ teaspoon sugar

Yuba rolls make an excellent and unusual hors d'oeuvre and are quick and simple to prepare. The first step involves either making the yuba or reconstituting frozen or air-dried yuba as shown on (pp.22-23). Set aside.

Next, wrap the tofu in a dry cloth to drain it of moisture, allow to stand for 20 minutes and then crumble. Combine all the ingredients in a bowl and knead thoroughly until smooth. Divide the tofu mixture into eight portions and spread evenly on the yuba sheets, leaving ¼in (6mm) edge on one side. Set aside. To ensure that the two sides of the yuba adhere, take a little cornflour, dissolve it in water and brush on the free yuba edge. Tightly roll the yuba towards the free edge.

To cook the yuba rolls, bring a steamer to a rolling boil. Place the yuba rolls in it, seam-side down and steam over a high heat for 20 minutes. Finally, remove the rolls, cut in half and serve immediately with shoyu and mustard.

STUFFED FRIED YUBA ROLLS

4 sheets of fresh or reconstituted yuba (4in x 5in, 10cm x 12.5cm)

For filling:
Boiled gingko nuts, ground meat with minced onions, grated cheese, cooked minced sausages, bacon and tomatoes etc.
Salt
Salad oil for deep-frying
1 egg white, well-beaten

Crispy yuba rolls with a variety of fillings, make a delicious hors d'oeuvre or snack.

To prepare, cut the yuba sheets in halves. Place a tablespoonful of the different fillings in the centre of each yuba slice. Fold each corner into the centre like an envelope and then roll into a slim stick. Moisten the roll flap with egg white.

When prepared, set the rolls aside seam-side down. Heat the salad oil in a frying pan and deep-fry the rolls until crisp. Drain well.

Arrange the rolls decoratively on a platter, sprinkle with a little salt and serve hot.

An exotic hors d'oeuvre or tasty snack Steamed or fried yuba rolls can be filled with a variety of delicious fillings.

INDEX